1983

Income Support Policies for the Aged

Income Support Policies for the Aged

edited by

G.S. Tolley
Richard V. Burkhauser

Ballinger Publishing Company • Cambridge, Massachusetts
A Subsidiary of J.B. Lippincott Company

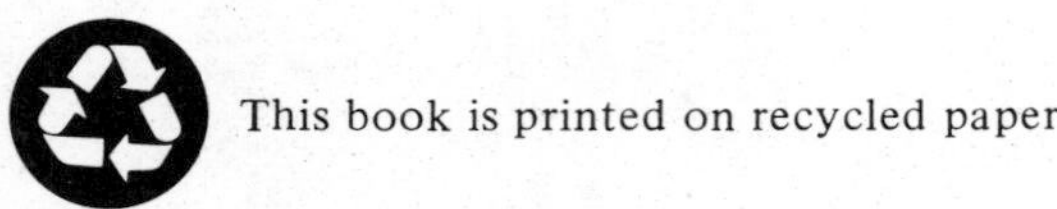

This book was prepared with the partial support of NSF Grant No. GI–39041. Any opinions, findings, conclusions, or recommendations herein are those of the authors and do not necessarily reflect the views of NSF.

International Standard Book Number: 0–88410–359–5

Library of Congress Catalog Card Number: 77–4155

Printed in the United States of America

Library of Congress Cataloging in Publication Data

Conference on Income Support Policies for the Aging,
University of Chicago, 1976.
Income support policies for the aged.

"The chapters in this book were originally presented at the Conference on Income Support Policies for the Aging at the University of Chicago, May 21, 1976."

1. Old age pensions—United States—Congresses. 2. Social Security—United States—Congresses. 3. Income maintenance programs—United States—Congresses. I. Tolley, George S., 1925– II. Burkhauser, Richard V. III. Title.
HD7106.U5C62 1976 368.4'3'00973 77–4155
ISBN 0–88410–359–5

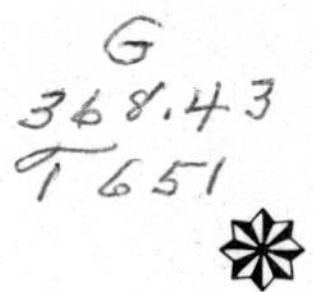

Contents

List of Contributors

Richard V. Burkhauser, Institute for Research on Poverty, University of Wisconsin, Madison, on leave to Office of Income Security Policy, Dept. of HEW

Robert Harris, The Urban Institute

Werner Z. Hirsch, University of California—Los Angeles

Charles D. Hobbs, Charles D. Hobbs, Inc.

Arthur B. Laffer, University of Chicago

Theodore R. Marmor, University of Chicago

Nelson McClung, Office of Tax Analysis, Department of the Treasury

Marilyn Moon, University of Wisconsin—Milwaukee

James N. Morgan, Institute for Social Research, University of Michigan

John L. Palmer, The Brookings Institution

R. David Ranson, University of Chicago

James H. Schulz, Brandeis University

Lawrence T. Smedley, Department of Social Security, AFL–CIO

Eugene Smolensky, University of Wisconsin—Madison

Lawrence H. Thompson, Office of Income Security Policy, Department of HEW

Robert Tilove, Martin E. Segal Company

G.S. Tolley, University of Chicago

Robin Jane Walther, Andrus Gerontology Center, University of Southern California—Los Angeles

Preface

A reconsideration of policies toward the aged is occurring under the economic pressures of a growing aged population. Social security, in the midst of both a short and a long term fiscal crisis, is subject to more criticism now than at any time in its history. This book considers social security within the totality of income support programs directed toward the aged. Present approaches are both severely attacked and vigorously defended by the contributors to the book and alternative solutions are suggested.

The book addresses fundamental issues including the proper measure of poverty for the aged and the role social security should play in providing for the poor. The affects of government on work, retirement, private pension participation, and saving for old age are examined.

The material in the book was originally presented at the Conference on Income Support Policies for the Aged at the University of Chicago, May 21, 1976. While the issues discussed center on economics, the book is an outgrowth of a broader interdisciplinary investigation of the aged initiated by Professor Bernice Neugarten of the Committee on Human Development of the University of Chicago. Her knowledge of and sensitivity to the problems of the aged have been of great aid.

We owe special thanks to Adele Wick who monitored the discussion of the participants and converted it into readable form. We also thank Gerry Young for her typing assistance.

Introduction

Diverse viewpoints on the type of support government should provide people in the later stages of life are presented in this book. The growth of social security benefits and taxes has increased public interest in the overall effects of the social security program. Too often, however, support or criticism of social security has been confined to one particular aspect of the system with little attempt to follow through the effects of the point of controversy on the system as a whole or, more importantly, on the welfare of individuals and ultimately on society as a whole.

Contributors to this volume were asked not to confine themselves to a single aspect of social security policy or even to social security itself, but rather to look at the total effect of government policy on the aged and on the young as they planned for older age. They were asked to suggest the directions of change in a broad way necessary to improve the current system of income support of the aged.

While no consensus was reached, there were some points of agreement. The emphasis and direction of the papers vary, and they elucidate the major issues which account for the sharpness of the debate over social security. A major purpose of the book is to clarify and advance this debate.

VIEWS EXPRESSED IN THE PAPERS

James Schulz begins in Chapter 1 by emphasizing the mixed nature of the present pension system. While acknowledging the problems of social security, he believes it will and should remain the major source of retirement income. He is especially critical of the apparent imbalance by economists in analyzing the pension system. Pointing out several potential problems surrounding equity and the total economic impact if private pensions are allowed to grow at the expense of social security, he calls for greater economic analysis of the consequences of enlarging these plans.

Robert Tilove agrees that social security should continue to be the primary bases of retirement income. He feels that means-tested programs like SSI (Supplementary Security Income) should continue to be residual in nature, with the redistributive aspects of social security remaining. However, he suggests redistribution could be within a two-layer system, a demogrant of $100 to every retired person, and a second layer of benefits based on previous earnings.

Marilyn Moon and Eugene Smolensky believe that if social security is regarded chiefly as a means of redressing sharp reductions in income, then the definition of income must be an accurate measure of need. They build a case for the inadequacy of current money income as a proper indicator and suggest a broader measure of economic status. This would include asset ownership, the value of time, and private and public transfers.

Robin Walther would expand the measure of economic status to include the health of individuals and would caution researchers who use empirical measures to specify the theoretical definition of economic well-being on which they are based.

George Tolley and Richard Burkhauser believe it is time to reevaluate the role social security should play within a broader system of income support. The advent of SSI removes much of the need for the crude redistributive aspects of social security. They suggest that private and public pensions should be treated equally under a tax system based on consumption-tax criteria. In the long run, a scaled down social security system, acturially based, might be made voluntary above some minimum with all anti-work bias removed.

Larry Thompson suggests that realistically the current social security system will change very little in the next 25 years, and that calls for major reform will go unheeded. In looking at the interaction of social security and SSI, he provides evidence that SSI has effectively removed the scaling of social security benefits for workers with a low earnings history. This in effect removes any relationship between contributions and benefits for this group.

Nelson McClung provides an overview on the net effect of government programs. He contends that estimating the incidence of any single government program is exceedingly complex, but suggests several issues policy-makers should turn to. Among these are the tax treatment of savings and the changes in labor-force participation of older workers resulting from ending the work test or increasing the normal retirement age.

James Morgan is in favor of retaining the earned right concept of social security. Each generation must be guaranteed benefits that reflect their tax expenditures plus an adequate rate of return, which he estimates to be a 3 percent real rate. He then provides estimates of lifetime savings rates necessary to provide such a return.

Arthur Laffer and David Ranson assert that social security has raised expectations of benefits that cannot be met by future generations. This inevitable broken promise they believe is the real moral issue, not the often-quoted tradeoff between equity and efficiency. They estimate the present unfunded liability of the system to have increased by 900 percent in the last 6 years, and that it currently is near $2.7 trillion.

Lawrence Smedley argues that the issue of unfunded liability is spurious. He cites the twentieth-century German experience with its wars, depression, and inflation as an example of the ability of social security to withstand economic adversity. The important point for economists to realize is that social security is simply not an economic institution but is a response by Congress to public pressure and it remains popular because it fits in with these demands.

John Palmer agrees that a funding problem is inevitable. He argues that some form of general revenue financing is the best short-run solution and that the presence of SSI might allow a more limited future role for social security in a broader system of support for the aged. But he argues that the unfunded liability is not a major threat to the system and feels that funds need not be in excess of those necessary to provide a cushion against temporary shortfalls of revenue relative to committed benefits.

Charles Hobbs believes that the present social security benefit scheme will not change, even given the increased economic pressure the system faces. Additional taxes must be raised, but he contends that any attempt to use general revenue financing will remove the best check on unwarranted increases in benefits. He feels it is only the countervailing pressure against increases in the payroll tax that can stop the political pressure toward ever-increasing benefits.

Robert Harris and Theodore Marmor agree that changes in the benefit structure are necessary in developing a specific program of long-run change. The role of women has altered and the old system of benefits based on presumptive need should be reviewed. But they are wary of the economists' view of the process of political change. They believe the political forces underlying change must be explicitly addressed before real change can be accomplished.

Werner Hirsch calls for a carefully developed rationale for an income-support policy for the aged. He is of the opinion that the conflict between individual equity and social adequacy is at the heart of much of the debate, but that only by addressing this conflict can the efficiency losses connected with poorly integrated government programs be minimized.

VIEWS EXPRESSED IN CONFERENCE DISCUSSIONS

The foregoing highlights some of the ideas appearing in the chapters of this book. A synopsis of the discussion raised by these papers when they were initially presented follows. Schulz cautioned economists for criticizing social security and recommending its decline or demise before careful scrutiny of the chief alternative—private pensions—has been undertaken. He asserted that the growth of private coverage has slowed considerably, leaving half of the working population uncovered. Additionally, the private sector has not been able to come up with an inflation hedge—the stock market has been unsatisfactory in this regard, with the possible exception of dividend payments. Another problem is that of vesting and portability. Labor mobility is hampered, and the hiring of older workers who are less likely to quit or die before pension-benefit retirement time is discouraged. Federal social security avoids these problems; its pay-as-you-go financing enables the indexing of benefits, and its coverage is national, not tied to occupation or location.

Tilove gave the following practical defense of private pensions. Variety has a positive value, if society can afford it. Private plans can break out of the mold and be innovative; furthermore, they aid in the dispersion of power. While not prepared to call private pensions models of democratic government, Tilove finds some value in the dispersion of the power of oligarchs against an all-powerful monarch, even if that monarch has been democratically elected.

Marilyn Moon and Eugene Smolensky build a powerful case for the gross inadequacy of current money income as a proper indicator. Imputed nonmoney flows (from, say, owner-occupied housing) and grants-in-kind (with a downward adjustment, perhaps, because of the diminished range of their substitutability) are important sources of attainable consumption. The more relevant target is this command over resources, better measured by concepts of human capital and permanent income. Differentiation of income by source is not helpful in this regard, nor need be the use of age as a criterion for benefit eligibility. Income declines are greater for the aged, but the purpose and focus should be on maintaining income standards—properly measured—rather than on age *per se*. To this, Robin Walther replied that age is a characteristic inexpensive to spot and expensive to manufacture artificially; alternative rationing devices such as assets and earnings tests might prove more costly to administer. She criticized Moon and Smolensky for neglecting the importance and uncertainty of health in their efforts to come closer to a true measure of welfare.

Moon and Smolensky contend that programs should consider the individual as a whole. This means that a program designed to insure against drastic falls in income from whatever source should not focus on money wage income exclusively, nor on age, nor on the retirement test. Given, however, that social security is financed by a payroll tax, then it should be viewed as insuring only wage income, and not property income typically unaffected by retirement. Moreover, if it is an insurance program and not an annuity or savings account program, as Tilove observes, the efficacy of social security should in only a minor way be tested by an "equity" test relating contributions to benefits. The better criterion is a replacement ratio. Furthermore, in principle, if the contingency insured against does not obtain, neither do the benefits accrue; hence the need for a work test.

But which measure of income should be the denominator of this ratio? Schulz suggested some average of the best ten of the last fifteen years. James Morgan criticizes this suggestion. Consider two people, *A* and *B*, who contribute the same totals to the program, *A* with a flat earnings path, *B* with a rising one. Under Schulz's scheme, *B* would receive greater benefits than *A*. This, he contends, violates any common man's notions of equity; and its avoidance is one of the points of using a measure of permanent income.

On this issue of horizontal equity, the desirability of equal treatment of equals, everyone concurred. The difficulty, however, lies in the definition of equality. Are Messrs. *A* and *B* equal? One firm area of agreement was that discriminatory treatment based on sex and marital status exists now, but should not, and indeed will not, exist much longer, being rapidly corrected by law.

For Tolley, the goal is to make the income distribution more equitable, for which objective replacement ratios are irrelevant success criteria. To effect this goal, the individual as a whole, not just as a present or past worker, should be considered, and the work test should be abolished.

This debate over the desirability of the work test was perhaps the second most spirited object of discussion. To Morgan, one's policy preferences on this matter depend on a view of our older citizens. If they are a homogeneous lot, eliminating the test is all right; but for a heterogeneous group, such elimination involves a transfer to the healthy, who receive social security and wage incomes, exacerbating welfare inequality.

Does the retirement test in fact affect people's work decisions? Emphatically yes, according to Burkhauser. The median worker eligible for social security benefits faces a marginal tax rate of over 70 percent. As replacement rates increase, this distortion of the work/leisure retirement choice becomes even more dramatic. The percentage of males aged 62–64 participating in the work force has declined from about 80 percent in 1962 to 70 percent in 1971 to about 60 percent in 1976. This to a large extent is the result of the eligibility of the group for early social security benefits. Most studies which report the choice between entering and not entering the work force as insensitive to wages, deal with the prime age work force. The response of marginal groups such as the aged is far more sizable.

Smedley is sceptical—he would like to see more hard data. Most people do not even know what a work test is, and the articulate minority who do have distorted the economists' perspective. Moreover, low-income earners can work full time and continue to collect benefits. According to Morgan, "Lots of people don't have posh jobs like us, but crummy jobs. Ask them, 'What do you miss about your job?' and they'll reply, 'Nothing—I miss not eating!' " With an 8–9 percent rate of unemployment, does public policy want to keep older people in the work force at the expense of women and teenagers?

To Tolley, the important statement is not that everybody wants to work, but that some would like to continue with their jobs. Why not give everyone the freedom of undistorted choice?

The answer, to Schulz, is the cost. The effect of having benefits flow to these presently disqualified people (estimated to be over one million) will not be inconsequential. The issue is whether the return of workers back into the labor force will be large enough to offset in any meaningful way this additional budgetary demand with the payroll taxes to which they will then be subject. Such an experiment being imperfectly amenable to hypothetical questioning, we shall probably never know, but Schulz's impression, boldly and baldly, is "No."

Thompson argues that the point of social security is precisely to enable people to retire. The proper goal as he sees it is to maximize welfare, not GNP. To Smedley also the importance of the retirement test has been grossly exaggerated. Its termination, however, would make social security much more costly; and given the financial trouble in which the program is presently embroiled, would not be the best use of resources.

Ranson asserts that the real cost is in the existence of the retirement test, not in its removal. Such high marginal tax rates drive retired people away from the work force and speed the process of aging. Moreover, the method of financing the program, a payroll tax, is even more costly. It taxes work and subsidizes nonmarket activity, inserting a wedge between the wage as viewed by employer and as perceived by employee. To him, the issue of who really pays the tax is secondary: "A transfer I would never view as a cost." Burkhauser contended that the issue is the difference between a transfer and a cost in a welfare sense. Money which the social security system pays out in benefits are a "cost" to the system, but to society as a whole it is merely a transfer from one group to another. But if a worker leaves the work force because of the tax on work inherent in the social security system, the loss in production is a cost to society which nobody gains.

Ranson is interested in the horizontal axis, quantity of labor employed, and not in the tax burden or incidence. Unambiguously, total labor input will fall; unambiguously, this is a net social loss. In a private insurance system, there are no incentive problems. Benefits are tied directly to contributions; indeed, they are equal at the margin; netting out, they have no disincentive effects. With a pay-as-you-go approach, this link is broken.

Tolley notes that social security benefits are tax exempt, while taxes paid into social security cannot be considered as deferred income for tax purposes. This is the opposite of the way private pensions are treated. This conflict between the treatment of private savings and social security savings should be eliminated. Our treatment of private pensions indicates a movement toward a consumption, instead of income, tax approach. One is taxed when one's income on savings is spent, not earned. Savings in a sense being deferred income, this move is a good one and should be adopted for social security. Moreover, social security now has all the attributes of a tax shelter for the upper-income strata, with all the vertical inequities therefrom. Social security should be integrated fully into the overall tax system.

Ranson, perceiving that people are still using private pension plans in spite of this tax discrimination, finds only two possible explanations: either the private pensioners are irrational or they doubt that the promised future social security benefits will be forthcoming. Irrationality being the first refuge of the economist who knows nothing, he opts for the latter. He contends that the social security program as it exists promises to a very vulnerable sector of society benefits it can deliver only with a probability close to zero. With this program, the U.S. government has amassed a liability of $2.7 trillion; in every substantive sense this is part of government debt more conventionally measured.

The deficiency has grown to a magnitude dominating considerations of incentives and economic drag, overwhelming anything else. In ten or fifteen years, if the same pace continues, no institution or entity in the world will be able to bail it out. One can only hope that the credibility of its promises will be so weakened that the aged will not be fooled.

The controversy surrounding the importance of the unfunded liability and its effects on capital accumulation was the most heated of the day. Martin Feldstein's work has indicated the deleterious effect of social security on saving and capital accumulation, two elements which tell no small part of the story of economic growth, according to Tolley. Smedley feels the whole issue is a spurious one. He believes the analogy with private insurance or even with private pensions is a false one. "Unfunded liability" is an actuarial term quite distinct from "unsound," and most actuaries would concur that the program is sound. Should we be concerned? Look at Germany, whose oldest social security system on record has survived two world wars, a hyperinflation, and a depression, and remains liberal and generous. Few worried about whether or not this program was properly funded while many of the government institutions around it were crumbling. Moreover, the present way in which the U.S. program is financed permits the inflation indexing of benefits. Were we to amend our formulas for adjusting for inflation, decoupling to prevent the present overcompensation, the size of the liability would be halved.

Smedley and Ranson would agree that from a strictly financial standpoint, it is not the existence of an unfunded liability *per se* which is worrisome. Ranson is, rather, concerned with a demographic change in which the retired population will be growing faster than the working population whose payroll taxes must finance the benefit bulge.

This point is made most cogently by Palmer in the context of the vertical equity issue. Palmer thinks that the size of the long-term liability is important, but only imperfectly predictable. It does seem clear that the potential conflict between the goals of individual equity (receiving the market rate of return on this forced saving) and social adequacy (redistributing income by the program) is about to become an actual one. Before, because of the combined effects on contributions of increased coverage of a growing labor force (proportionate to the senior citizen population), benefits grew amply enough to redistribute income without sacrificing individual equity. This happy situation cannot continue, and the two goals will be from now on in conflict. The social adequacy or welfare component—the redistribution of income—will become politically difficult to finance by the sacrifices of individual equities.

Thompson noted that the unfunded nature of the liability in the context of demographic change precludes making participation in the social security program voluntary—we cannot have Tolley's freedom of choice. Those with high incomes, whose individual equity would be sacrificed, would opt out and substitute toward private pension coverage. This political pressure is already visible among certain unions and, indeed, among various civil servants in the public sector itself. Moreover, as noted by Ranson, the subsidization of nonmarket and taxation of market activity acts to exacerbate the decline in the rate of growth of one component of the taxable base, the labor force. More taxes are unpopular even when tied directly to increased benefits, one must ask, and How could the political will be generated to raise them for the benefit of totally unrelated population groups? How much will other sources of growth, such as technological progress, compensate for this decline and for that of capital accumulation?

To Smedley, the burden simply does not exist to the extent implied by Laffer and Ranson. The issue is not really about the increasing percentage of older people and the decreasing percentage of workers supporting them. The issue is really about workers supporting nonworkers who exist in any society.

While the solutions offered differ, most of the participants favor facing the coming problems of maintaining an income support system for older people on the basis of fundamental principles rather than ad hoc remedies.

 *Chapter 1*

Public Policy and the Future Rolls of Public and Private Pensions

James H. Schulz

It is now about a century since the first comprehensive plan of social insurance was established in Germany and the first company pension plans were established in the United States. The U.S. Civil Service Retirement Act of 1920 and the Social Security Act of 1935 mark a half century of federal government involvement in pension legislation.

In discussing how best to provide adequate economic support in old age, we cannot ignore the political and economic reality of the existing pension programs that have developed over the years. As we know from watching television or reading the morning and evening newspapers, income security (or income maintenance) has become "big business" for both the private and public sectors. While debates over programs providing individuals with economic support to supplement or supplant earned income have always been spirited, today we see the battle lines hardening with an intensity which equals or surpasses previous periods.

The two major factors which are probably responsible for the rising intensity of the debates are, first, the burgeoning costs of the various existing programs and, second, the increased stake of various parties in the outcomes of the income security issues before us. As Friedman and Hausman have pointed out in an excellent discussion of what they characterized as "welfare in retreat," there has been an unplanned, somewhat accidental, mushrooming of *income-conditioned* welfare benefits and the number of people who receive these

An earlier draft of this paper was read by Robert Ball, Barry L. Friedman, Leonard J. Hausman, and Nelson McClung; consequently, this version has benefited from their comments.

benefits (Friedman and Hausman, 1977). Between fiscal years 1968 and 1975, cash public assistance recipients rose from about 9 to 16 million; Medicaid recipients increased from 11.5 to over 25 million; and Food Stamp recipients went from 2.5 to 19 million (an incredible sixfold increase). The result has been a doubling of real federal expenditures on income-conditioned programs from $14.5 billion to over $29 billion in 1973 prices.

In the health area, skyrocketing medical expenditures, including those for Medicare and Medicaid, have caused some people working in the health field to describe our medical system as economically out of control. And in the area of the focus of this paper—retirement pensions—expenditures have now reached very high levels. In 1973 (the latest year of available data for all programs) over $79 billion in retirement benefits were paid out by the private and public sectors (see Table 1–1).

One result of this growth in social welfare programs is a *significant improvement in the economic welfare of the aged.* Another result is that the scope of individual and family discretion and responsibility for old-age economic security has narrowed considerably over the years. And probably of equal importance is the result that the stake of individuals in the outcomes of the pension policy discussions underway today is much greater than in the early 1930s and 1940s—when these programs were in their infancy and self-reliance was still the watchword.

Moreover, the stake of private firms in the outcomes has also increased significantly. Over the past three decades the management of private retirement pension funds has exploded into a $200 billion

Table 1–1. Pension Expenditures, 1973 *(in billions of dollars)*

	Assets	*Benefits*
OASI benefits		43.7
Private pension and deferred profit-sharing plan benefits		11.2
Contributions paid into pension reserves	21.1	
Pension reserves, book value	180.2	
Federal employee pension benefits		9.7
Veterans' pensions and compensation		6.4
State and local government pension plan benefits		5.5
Railroad retirement benefits		2.6
Benefit total		79.1

Sources: Kolodrubetz, 1975; Dales, 1974; "Current Operating Statistics, 1975.

industry. The smaller disability insurance industry also continues to grow steadily. Together they represent a large and powerful interest group.

The time has come for us to give more attention to the future mix of private and public sector involvement in income security provision. And, hence, this paper selects from the range of pension financing, adequacy, and equity issues which are currently under discussion, those issues that seem most relevant for deciding what the appropriate mix of public and private long-term income security programs should be. The main focus of the paper, therefore, is to examine a number of problems resulting from the current mix of pensions and to suggest alternative directions for reform.

THE RESULTS OF PENSION DEVELOPMENT

The growth of pensions in the United States has produced a number of significant developments. Two are of particular importance:

1. The improving economic status of the retired elderly.
2. A disparity in pension coverage and pension income adequacy.

The most common way of assessing the economic status of the elderly is by using the Census Bureau's data on money income and comparing income levels to a poverty index or the Bureau of Labor Statistics's "Retired Couples' Budget." Such assessments suffer from a variety of limitations, as follows.

1. Persons or families with full-time or part-time workers are mixed with nonworkers, making it difficult to assess the economic status of *the retired.*
2. Assets and nonmoney income are not taken into account.
3. There is significant underreporting of income, especially transfer income, in the surveys.
4. They ignore the special tax exemptions of the elderly—such as the exemption of social security income, the double personal exemption, and favorable property tax treatment—that increase their after-tax income relative to the non-aged.

But even without adjusting for these limitations in the data, we find rapid improvement in the economic status of the elderly—with 30 percent of aged persons, for example, below the official poverty level in 1967 as compared to 16 percent in 1974 (see also Schulz, 1976a).

Perhaps more significant for the economic status of the *future* elderly population is the emerging pattern of pension coverage. It has proved to be a relatively easy matter in all countries to extend social security coverage to large segments of the labor force. Coverage of agricultural workers and the self-employed has presented certain problems—especially in developing countries—but, in general, extension of coverage all over the world has been quite comprehensive.

In the United States, social security coverage has been extended over the years. In 1973, for example, 90 percent of those in paid employment were covered—with the bulk of those not covered being government employees covered by alternative plans. In contrast, extension of private pension coverage presents serious problems.

It is especially difficult to extend private pension coverage among small employee groups. Among the factors that have been cited for this difficulty are:

1. The high costs per employee of establishing and maintaining a private plan.
2. The lack of pressure in some companies from employees or unions.
3. The fact that small business firms are often relatively young and, on average, short-lived.
4. The fact that small employers tend to view pensions as personal costs.
5. The personality of small business owners who tend to emphasize individual self-reliance in financial matters.
6. The often unstable and insecure financial status of many small businesses and the competitive pressures for cost-cutting.

As a result of these and other factors, a sizable proportion of the work force in countries with private pensions are not likely to be covered by such pensions.

In fact, this is the actual case in the United States. Unfortunately, estimates of private pension coverage are subject to a wide margin of error. Recent estimates for the United States of the proportion of private sector earners covered have varied from 35 to 50 percent. The best study thus far available is for full-time employees only (in 1972) and reports 47 percent coverage—with coverage for men being 52 percent and coverage for women being much lower at 36 percent (Kolodrubetz and Landay, 1973). Based on this study and other information, the Social Security Administration estimates that 44 percent of private wage and salary workers were covered by private pension in 1973.

Table 1–2 shows how pension coverage in the United States varies

Table 1–2. Private Pension Coverage, April 1972

Wage and salary workers in private industry	*Percent*
All full-time and part-time employees	43.7%
Full-time employees only	47.0
Men	52.0
Women	36.0
Whites	48.0
Non-whites	39.0
Full-time employees, by industry:	
Communications and public utilities	82
Mining	72
Manufacturing	
Durable goods	63
Nondurable goods	57
Finance, insurance, and real estate	52
Transportation	45
Trade	
Wholesale	48
Retail	31
Construction	34
Services	29
Full-time employees, by earnings	
Men earning less than $5,000	26
Women earning less than $5,000	31
Men earning $5,000–9,999	58
Women earning $5,000–9,999	58

Source: Kolodrubetz, 1974; Kolodrubetz and Landay, 1973.

by work status, sex, race, industry, and earnings. Part-time workers, women, nonwhites, and low earners have the lowest coverage. The industries with the lowest coverage are service, wholesale and retail trade, and construction.

One result of the differences in the mix of pension coverage for various workers is wider differences in pension income. Many people reaching retirement age must rely solely on the social security system for their pension income. Others receive both social security and a private pension. Still others receive a public service pension, with a large number of former government employees also achieving eligibility for social security by a combination of pre-government employment, second jobs, or post-government employment.[1]

A study by the Social Security Administration, for example, provides information on the ratio of pension income to preretirement earnings of males becoming entitled to social security retirement benefits in early 1970. Table 1–3 shows the dramatic difference in

1. The U.S. Joint Economic Committee estimated in 1973, for example, that 40 percent of all civil service pensioners also received social security pensions. Some of these government workers who shift to the private sector also receive private pensions and thus have three major pensions!

Table 1–3. Pensions as a Percent of Estimated Preretirement Earnings for Male Workers Achieving Entitlement in Early 1970

	Men Receiving		
Replacement[a] Rate (percent)	*Social Security Pension Only, Earnings Below Maximum (percent)*	*Social Security Pension Only, Earnings At or Above Maximum (percent)*	*Social Security and a Private Pension (percent)*
Number[b]	61,800	31,500	64,800
0–20	1	21	1
21–30	21	68	6
31–40	45	11	19
41–50	15	0	28
51–60	5	0	23
61–70	4	0	13
71 or more	10	0	11
Median	36	24	49

[a]Social security benefits and private pensions as a percent of total earnings in the three years of highest earnings in the ten years before award; percentage distribution of wage and salary workers entitled to benefits payable at award or at time of survey, January–June 1970.

[b]Excludes not only persons with less than three years earnings in last ten years, but also those who were self-employed in their longest job, who were receiving public employee pensions, or who failed to report the amount of private pensions. Also excluded are those whose earnings attained the taxable maximum in the first or second quarter of any of the three highest years.

Source: Fox, 1974.

replacement rates between workers with only social security and those with two pensions.

PROBLEMS OF A MIXED PENSION SYSTEM

Pension programs were established, in large part, as a reaction to the inability or unwillingness of a large number of individuals to provide satisfactorily for their old age through personal saving (Schulz, 1976b). They were also a response to general dissatisfaction with the network of family and welfare support mechanisms that had to be introduced to moderate the resulting economic destitution. The establishment of pension programs to meet these problems, however, has created some new problems related to pension financing and equity.

A number of the problems arising in connection with pension programs in the United States are directly related to or exacerbated by the fact that we have a *mixed* pension system. Instead of one pension program together with personal saving to provide for old age, three distinctive types of programs have evolved: (1) government employee pensions; (2) occupational/industrial pensions; and (3) social security.[2] It is the existence of this multiple-pension system with its interaction among programs and a high degree of nonintegration that accounts for some of the problems or costs we now face in our attempts to provide collectively for old age.

Overshooting and Undershooting Benefit Targets

Economic provision for old age requires planning years in advance, given the magnitude of the task (see Schulz and Carrin, 1972). With a mixed pension system, for example, the magnitude of targeted private pension benefits are not independent of social security benefit levels. Yet benefit levels must be set by two different decision-making bodies (Congress and labor/management), without either being sure of the future pension benefits of the other.

Attempts to devise private pension formulas that take account of changes in social security have not been very successful. "Excess plans" that begin to provide benefits above certain compensation levels or higher benefits above certain levels (step-rate plans) were quite common in the 1950s. Usually these formulas established a

2. Some might add to the list—given their increasing popularity—deferred profit-sharing retirement plans. We do not extensively discuss government employee plans. An excellent and up-to-date discussion of government employee pensions and their distinctive characteristics can be found in Tilove (1976).

"step" at the social security taxable earnings ceiling. But frequent past changes in this ceiling and the discussions of possible large future changes made private pension planning difficult. The step levels in most plans quickly became obsolete as the social security base moved from $3,000 to $14,000 (in 1975), and consequently the use of such formulas declined dramatically. "Offset plans" that deduct social security benefits from the benefits that would otherwise be payable under private plans have also become unpopular. The explicit, and hence very visible, reduction of benefits in offset plans, as social security benefits increase, causes a strong feeling among employees that past compensation gains (bargained collectively or individually) are being lost through decisions over which they have little control.

A very serious problem has arisen because of the lack of integration of government employee plans with other pensions. Government employees have been able to pyramid pension benefits by shifting, after achieving pension eligibility, from government employment to a job that permits them to achieve eligibility for social security and possibly also a private pension (see *Reports of the Quadrennial Advisory Council*, 1975).

A different problem arises from the vesting provisions of the various pension plans. The broad coverage of social security practically eliminates loss of pension credits when workers change jobs. Only if workers shift permanently into noncovered employment (primarily government jobs) before achieving fully insured status can they in effect lose accumulated credits (and related contributions). But given the relatively narrow coverage of any particular private plan, loss of accumulated credits is much more frequent.

Most private plans require a minimum number of years of credited employment before vesting benefits. Federal regulation of private pensions (ERISA) provides options requiring full vesting after no more than 10–15 years. With frequent job changes typically occurring during the early years of a worker's career, less frequent changes in the later years, and the possibility of involuntary termination due to mergers, bankruptcy, and the like, occurring at any age—some workers invariably lose significant amounts of benefits and may fail to accumulate a sizable supplement to social security despite their working many years in firms with private pensions.

And for those who change jobs after achieving vested benefits, another problem arises. Vested private pension benefits are not adjusted upward if the pension plan's formula for *continuing* workers is changed either to compensate for inflation or to provide a higher level of real benefits.

Labor-Force Impact

Over the years concern has been raised over the impact of pension plans on labor mobility. In particular there has been a fear that the vesting provisions of private pensions might discourage workers from shifting jobs (U.S. Department of Labor, 1964). In fact, pension plans were sold to many employers in the 1940s and 1950s as a device for reducing labor turnover.

While we would not expect the accumulation of pension rights to *dominate* the job decision-making process of younger workers, does it have any significant effect? Until recently there was almost no research on this issue. Recently, however, an analysis of the job-change behavior of 60,000 workers covered by private pensions in 177 large firms "clearly demonstrates that private pension plans are an important institutional determinant of labor supply and utilization patterns." In general, it was found that:

> the promise of vesting or (early) retirement eligibility or the promise of higher retirement benefit levels tends to increase firm attachment (reduce exit) among those who are approaching such status, while the attainment of retirement eligibility and the immediate availability of higher retirement benefits tends to diminish attachment (increase exit) among affected workers. . . . What this implies is that the labor mobility requirement for productive efficiency may be seriously constrained by the institutional phenomenon of private pension plans. [Schiller and Weiss, 1975.]

A different sort of labor problem arises in connection with older workers. With the growth of private pensions has come the recognition that the existence of this fringe benefit in the pay package may represent a potential barrier of substantial magnitude to the employment of older workers (Schulz, 1975). Management may be reluctant to hire older workers because it is usually more costly to provide such workers with a specified pension benefit. This higher cost results primarily from three factors: (1) a shorter work history over which employer pension contributions must be made; (2) a lower probability of employee withdrawal, disability, or death between hiring and retirement; and (3) lower investment income arising from the pension contributions. In a rather old (but the only) published government study investigating the magnitude of this cost differential, Murray W. Latimer (1965), found for selected *hypothetical* private pension plans considerable variation in the cost differential—depending upon the assumed characteristics of these plans. He found, however, that in all cases it would cost more (in pension payments) to hire older workers.

This problem has been recognized in various countries, and a search for ways to avoid it has begun. Swedish unions, for example, have concluded an agreement with employers associations to develop and implement "age neutral" private pensions by the end of this year. In Great Britain the Trade Union Congress recently advised its bargaining units to resist pension provisions, such as a maximum entry age, that are prejudicial to older workers (*Occupational Pension Schemes*, 1976).[3]

Preliminary results from a study of American job-changers, using data from the 1972 *Current Population Survey*, indicate that job-changers age 45 and older have a significantly lower probability of private pension coverage in their new jobs. About 60 percent of job-changers ages 30 to 39 became covered in their new job, versus 53 percent for ages 45 to 54 and 37 percent for ages 55 to 59.[4] This occurs despite the fact that there is no apparent tendency for older job-changers to go into "low-coverage industries" in greater proportions than younger workers.

Problems of Coverage

As discussed above, private pensions presently cover less than half of the wage earners in the private sector. And, as we also noted, this large gap in coverage produces differences in total pension income available to people in their old age.

Another difference that results is the amount of individual discretion allowed for retirement preparation. Very few private pension plans in the United States make participation optional, and fewer still allow significant choices by participants in the nature and level of benefits (see Schulz, 1970).[5] Regardless of whether it is argued that more or less individual discretion is desirable (and both cases can be argued), the fact remains that there exists in the labor force a wide difference in the extent of *compulsory* retirement preparation as a result of the split in the working population between those covered by private pensions and those who are not.

In addition to the differences in pension income and compulsory

3. Under ERISA, newly hired workers over age 25 with one year of service cannot be denied admission to a plan. While ERISA contains a general prohibition against maximum age limits, workers hired within five years of the normal retirement age may be excluded from participation.

4. These findings are from a research project currently in process by the author, entitled "Barriers to the Employment of Older Workers," sponsored by the Ethel Percy Andrus Foundation.

5. The lack of options in this country contrasts with the situation in Canada where there are a large number of "contributory plans" with voluntary participation (76 percent). (See Statistics Canada, 1976.)

retirement preparation, there is yet another significant problem arising from irregular coverage. Tax legislation over the years, presumably to encourage the establishment of private pension plans, has permitted a variety of important exemptions that reduce the tax liabilities of covered employees. Employer contributions to qualified private pension and profit-sharing plans are excluded from the income of covered workers and are deducted by the employer as business expenses. In addition, the investment income arising from these pension plans is tax exempt.

The workers *not* covered by private pensions do not receive any of these tax benefits. And since general tax levels must be higher as a result of the revenue lost through this exemption, the provisions represent a major subsidy to *covered* workers—not only by the government but by those workers not covered by private pensions. Thus, a serious question of fairness arises when half the working population gets its future pensions generously subsidized by the other half.[6]

The amounts involved are certainly *not* inconsequential. The Congressional Budget Office estimates the revenue loss from the exclusion of pension contributions and earnings to be $6.5 billion in fiscal year 1977 ("Tax Expenditures," 1976). Also, given the fact that private pension coverage is greatest among middle- and upper-income taxpayers, the subsidy tends to go from lower-income taxpayers and their families to those in the upper-income classes. The Congressional Budget Office estimates that almost three-quarters of the tax exemptions benefit taxpayers with adjusted gross incomes of $15,000 or more.

Administrative Costs

Kenneth Boulding has argued the relevancy of administrative cost considerations in the design of pension policy as follows:

> The case for or against a government monopoly of insurance rests partly on questions of general preference for public as against private enterprise. It also rests on a certain matter of fact—whether or not there are important economies of scale in the insurance business. If there are these economies—that is, if the cost of administering the insurance declines with every increase in the amount of insurance written—then a state monopoly will almost inevitably be cheaper than a number of competing private compa-

6. The equity issue was one important reason for the recent federal legislation that permits employees not covered by private pension plans to deduct up to 15 percent of earned income (up to $1,500 a year) to be set aside free of taxation until subsequently paid out. The experience of Canada, however, strongly indicates that this provision will be used mainly by upper-income workers. See Schulz (1976b) for statistics on the Canadian experience.

> nies. If, on the other hand, costs begin to rise beyond a scale of operations that still permits a number of companies to occupy the field, the case for a state monopoly is much weaker. We may venture a hypothesis that where the operations of insurance are fairly routine, the case for state or national monopoly is stronger than where the operations involve great difficulties of *definition* of rights. Thus in Old Age and Survivors' Insurance it is usually a fairly routine matter to determine who should get how much in benefits: in the vast majority of cases the fact of death or of age is easily established by a doctor's certificate or a birth record. [Boulding, 1958.]

Although social security in the United States is far from being uncomplicated, there are many aspects of its operation which are structured relatively simply. As a consequence, the collection and benefit pay-out process permits the extensive use of computers. This in turn permits the handling of large numbers of claims in a way that allows significant economies of large-scale operation to be realized. In fiscal year 1974, for example, administrative expenses were only 1.5 percent of OASI payroll contributions.

In assessing the comparative costs between social security and private pensions, however, analysis is complicated by the fact that social security financing in the United States is on a pay-as-you-go basis, while private pensions are funded. Private pension funding costs generated as a result of *financial investment activities* carried out (usually) on behalf of employers have no analogous counterpart in the United States social security program.

Banks, insurance companies, unions, and corporations administer private pension plans. Although there has been no study of the comparative costs of private pension plans versus social security, it is difficult to imagine that the current conglomeration of thousands of private plans, many covering less than a hundred workers, can have lower administrative costs. A study by Caswell (1974), for example, of a representative sample of multi-employer plans in the construction industry, found that total administrative expenses averaged slightly less than 4 percent of current contributions and that significant economies of scale were associated with larger plans.

In addition, it has become clear in recent years that there is to be a large and growing administrative cost arising from the necessity of regulating and supervising private pension operations. The misuse of some pension funds, the loss of pensions and pension credits due to plan terminations, and excessive vesting requirements (among other things) produced strong political support in the early 1970s for more comprehensive federal regulation of private pensions. The Employees Retirement Income Security Act (ERISA) enacted in 1974 to regulate private pensions has been characterized by some as one of the most complicated pieces of legislation ever enacted in this country. It mandates major supervisory tasks to both the Department of Labor and the Treasury Department. It also establishes a new agency, the Pension Guarantee Corporation, to insure the pension credits of workers; its operations are financed through business payments paid to the new public corporation.

In addition to the taxpayer costs of the federal supervisory agencies and their staffs, considerable new regulatory costs are imposed on the businesses with pension funds. These costs arise from the necessity of providing information to the government in order that it can carry out its various supervisory roles. Because of the complexity of the new regulations, business must either develop staff or hire outside consultants to provide them with the expertise necessary to ensure compliance with the new law. Businesses have been complaining strongly before congressional committees both about the high costs of reporting required information to the government and also the costs of simply understanding the new law (see Lindsey, 1976).[7]

Given both the routine and supervisory costs associated with private pensions, there seems to be little doubt that in the years to come we will be paying (through lower wages and higher prices) a considerable amount to administer our private pension system. If reliance on private pensions increases as some suggest (for example, mandatory private pensions for all business), these costs will grow dramatically.

Of course, the existence of costs, even large costs, is not sufficient justification, by itself, to support a policy of reducing or eliminating any program. Rather, such costs must be weighed against the program's benefits, as well as the costs and benefits of alternative programs. In the case of pensions, we must ask ourselves what the benefits of private pensions are over social security (see below), what their relative costs are, and whether other options are both feasible and desirable (for example, greater reliance on personal provision for old age together with a negative income tax scheme).

Inflation Protection

Given that economic preparation for retirement and retirement living spans a lifetime, the impact of inflation over the long run be-

7. Since the enactment of ERISA, many pension plans (especially in small businesses) have been terminated because of the costs of complying with the new act. Studies by the Pension Guarantee Corporation indicate that adverse economic conditions accounted for a significant proportion of these terminations, but that 12 percent of terminations were due solely to ERISA and 34 percent partially involved ERISA.

comes an important concern. Will the value of funds invested 30 years before retirement at least maintain their real value into the retirement period? Will inflation during a 10- to 20-year retirement period significantly reduce the value of retirement income from savings, annuities, or pensions?

An argument frequently made in favor of public pensions is their ability, in contrast to private plans, to deal with the need for pensions to respond to inflation and economic growth. The problem of inflation has plagued pension programs since their inception. All countries have had to struggle with this problem, continually adjusting pension programs and benefits to offset increases in price levels. Inflation has varied, for example, from the catastrophic rate in early Germany (which completely wiped out the monetary value of that country's social security reserves and benefits) to the relatively mild price increases averaging less than 2 percent in the United States during the 1958–1968 period, to the more than 6 percent per year United States rate since 1968.

Gradually most industrialized countries (including the United States in 1972) have introduced some sort of automatic benefit adjustment mechanisms into the social security program to deal more effectively with the inflation problem (see Tracy, 1976). In contrast, private pension plans, with few exceptions, virtually ignore the need for regularized adjustment mechanisms. This results, in large part, because of employers' unwillingness to make financial commitments based on guesses about future price levels and the fear that the cost of these adjustments may be too high.

It is much easier for governments to deal with the inflation problem—given their inherent taxing powers and their ability to minimize the size of the monetary fund necessary to guarantee the financial soundness of the pension program. A pay-as-you-go system, for example, finds it easier to increase revenues to pay for inflation-adjusted wages because the earnings base is also rising with inflation. In contrast, many securities in a reserve fund will not adjust upward in value with the inflation.

The actual history of social security programs dealing with inflation in various countries supports this conclusion. Even after runaway inflations, countries have been able to adjust pensions to the new price level (see, for example, Rimlinger, 1971). In addition, public pension programs have shown an ability to devise equitable ways of permitting retired persons to share systematically in the real economic growth of the country. Social security programs in some countries—such as Belgium, Canada, Norway, and West Germany—provide for automatic or semiautomatic adjustments in *real* benefit levels. Still others adjust benefits systematically by various ad hoc processes.

THE GAINS FROM A MIXED PENSION SYSTEM

John McConnell has succinctly summarized a commonly voiced view of our mixed pension system:

> When the Social Security Act was passed, the purpose of old-age insurance was said to be the provision of a floor of income support. It was expected that individual savings would supplement the basic OASDI benefit. Following the rapid expansion of private pension plans during and following World War II, it became quite common for both the proponents and opponents of old-age insurance to refer to the American system of income maintenance as a three-legged stool, or a three-layer cake, although the pitiful nature of the income received by most older people from all sources made the analogy of the cake seem something of a mockery. It is quite clear that the spread of private pension plans has confused the role of OASDI and of private pensions and savings. There is a tendency to argue that OASDI should provide only minimum subsistence, and that private pensions will supply enough when added to OASDI to equal an adequate income. Private saving will assure a comfortable existence. ["Role of Public and Private Programs," 1968.]

Those writing about the growth of private pensions in the 1940s and thereafter have attributed this growth to a variety of factors:

1. Continued industrialization of the U.S. economy, together with a movement of workers out of agriculture, which stimulated increasing interest in alternatives other than the family for providing retirement security.
2. The introduction of private pensions by some employers as a way of creating employee loyalty and discouraging job shifting—since most early plans called for the worker to lose rights to the pension upon leaving the firm.
3. Wage freezes during World War II and the Korean War that encouraged fringe benefit growth in lieu of wages.
4. A series of favorable tax inducements offered by the federal government beginning with the Revenue Acts of 1921 and 1926. Probably the most important inducement was offered in the Revenue Act of 1942, coming at a time of sharp federal personal and corporate income tax increases.

5. A favorable decision by the Supreme Court in 1949 supporting the National Labor Relations Board's decision that pensions were a proper issue for collective bargaining.
6. The report of the Steel Industry Fact-Finding Committee in 1949, which included a recommendation that the industry had a social obligation to provide workers with pensions.
7. The development of multi-employer pension plans—particularly in the construction, transportation, trade, and service industries.
8. In the face of chronic unemployment, private pensions have become an increasingly popular mechanism for attempting to create jobs for younger workers by encouraging older worker retirement.
9. Growing recognition by unions of the inadequacy of social security benefits and the need for supplementation.

While there has been much support over the years for supplementing or supplanting personal provision for retirement by *both* public and private pension, there has been relatively little explicit discussion of the advantages of a mixed pension system. Over the years great emphasis has been placed on the desirability of keeping social security benefits to a minimum, but as observed by Derek Bok, "no clear explanation has been given to suggest just why the notion of a minimum floor [for social security] is appropriate or what sort of minimum is implied. As a result, the concept has meant all things to all men" ("Emerging Issues," 1967).

As indicated above, strong pressures and inducements arose to develop and expand private pensions. Underlying them all, however, were the facts (a) that social security pension levels in the early years were at poverty levels, and (b) that few people were willing or able to save for retirement. The fact that there existed a glaring gap between the income needs of the elderly and available economic resources must be viewed as a pervasive factor influencing the development of private pensions in the postwar years. Today, however, the two most common justifications voiced for private pensions are (a) their flexibility and diversity, and (b) their importance for capital formation.

Flexibility

On the one hand, a private pension can be a flexible management tool. As Charles A. Siegfried (1970) of the Metropolitan Life Insurance Company has observed, "a pension plan can be devised to attract and hold employees or it can be devised to facilitate the separation of employees from employment. On the other hand, pension objectives may vary to accommodate different employee wishes and aspirations, these being determined by decisions of the employers

(unilaterally or in consultation with workers) or by collective bargaining.

The late Edwin S. Hewitt, a well-known pension consultant, arguing the case for private pensions before the U.S. Senate Special Committee on Aging, emphasized the flexibility factor:

> . . . It is extraordinary how flexible an instrument for providing adequate security the private plan has proved to be. There are two kinds of flexibility and perhaps this fact is underrated when we oppose what private plans are doing.
>
> First, is their flexibility in terms of adapting to different needs. Very real differences in security problems exist among different companies, different industries, different age groups. . . .
>
> The second dimension is the flexibility between periods of time. Private plans have exhibited amazing flexibility to make their provisions meet the different needs that a group may have at different times.
>
> The initial job of most pension plans when first established is to concentrate on retirement income for the older worker, hence the importance of past service benefits. As plans become better funded, they tend to branch into other areas. Variety increases as plans are able to spend more money and give attention to tailor-made benefits to meet specific needs. [Hewitt, 1970.]

While the greater flexibility available from a decentralized group of pension plans (separately determined and administered) cannot be denied, one should not overemphasize the extent to which diversity is required. A much more restrictive view of the diversity attribute is contained in this statement by the British Trades Union Congress (1976):

> One of the main arguments put forward to support the existence of occupational pension schemes is their flexibility in meeting the different needs of groups of employees. However, needs will vary as much within a scheme as between schemes, and the only basic difference that can arise, in normal circumstances, between schemes is the need for an early retirement age in a few occupations such as the police or airline pilots. Even this difference can be quite easily dealt with with a single scheme. . . .

While the TUC's view of the need for diversity is perhaps too narrow, it is clear that much of the diversity that currently exists arises not so much from the special circumstances of particular employee groups, but because of differences in financial resources available for pension purposes. One is tempted to accept the existing diversity in coverage and comprehensiveness of provisions as the joint product of employer and worker decision-making about the magnitude of current versus future consumption. But in doing so, one is confronted with the very skewed nature of the outcome. Those without pension coverage and those covered by the worst private plans tend to be concentrated in low-pay occupations and industries and, hence, are most in need of income supplementation in their retirement. While it would not be surprising if low earners had very high rates of time preference (Thurow, 1973), it does not follow that public policy should remain neutral toward this fact or, for that matter, that public policy should not actively seek a different allocation of consumption over the life-cycle.

Pension Saving and Capital Formation

A much more controversial argument made in favor of private pensions is their role in the mobilization of national saving for economic investment. Charles Moeller, economist for the Metropolitan Life Insurance Company, has argued the case in this way:

> The key to any nation's economic growth is its ability to direct substantial portions of its output into real investment, i.e., to defer current consumption of output through saving and to permit investment in *productive* facilities for use in future production processes. . . . In effect, what pension funding operations and other forms of contractual saving do is to improve the efficiency and stability of the capital markets. . . .
>
> The importance of the saving function for private pension plans cannot be too strongly emphasized. The need for encouraging the accumulation of individual saving flows and of recirculating these funds back into the economy through the investment process has been spotlighted by the dramatic events of recent years including the "crunch" of 1966 and the "liquidity crisis" of 1970. ["The Role of Private Pension Plans," 1972.]

While there is no disagreement over the fact that there is a need for saving in an economy, there are a variety of ways such saving can be accumulated and, hence, there is no agreement on the need or importance of any one accumulation process—such as through private pensions. Clearly, economic growth through investment occurred in the United States during the years before significant private pension funds were accumulated. In the key growth sector of *corporate* production, the overwhelming majority of funds needed to finance new investment comes from the *internal* funds saved by the corporations themselves. "If you subtract housing investment from total capital investment funds, more than 99 percent of real capital investment funds took the form of corporate retained earnings or depreciation allowance in 1973" (Thurow, 1976). As John Kenneth Galbraith (1967) has observed, "The decisions on what will be saved are made in the main by a few hundred large corporations."[8] Moreover, other possible sources of saving are unincorporated businesses, individuals, and government budget surpluses.

If we limit the discussion to pensions as a source of saving, it should be noted that the generation of such savings is not limited to private pensions. Public social security reserve funds can also be generated. For example, the financing rates for the social security program in Sweden have been deliberately set high enough to help the chronic shortage of saving in the Swedish economy. Similarly, Martin Feldstein, concerned about evidence that indicates growing social security benefits may be reducing total personal savings, advocates a funded social security system (see his testimony in Subcommittee on Social Security, 1975).

Finally, we must remember that there currently exists considerable disagreement over both the need to promote growth and also the extent to which there is any insufficiency of saving in the United States relative to investment opportunities and the willingness of business to undertake investment. Regarding the latter issue, Arthur Okun, for example, has recently observed that "the specter of depressed saving is not only empirically implausible but logically fake. . . . The nation can have the level of saving and investment it wants with more or less [income] redistribution, so long as it is willing to twist some other dials (*Equality and Efficiency*, 1975; see also Bernstein, 1975; Wallich, 1975; Katona and Strumpel, 1976).

WHAT OPTIONS FOR THE FUTURE?

The prior two sections presented a brief discussion of various costs and gains associated with a mixed pension system such as we have in the United States. There are no obvious and "correct" conclusions that follow from such an exercise. The issues that exist, however, do indicate that we need to rethink the traditional three-legged stool concept of old-age income maintenance. The analogy does not fit well with the existing reality. But, more importantly, the growing magnitude of economic impacts and the growing complexity of institutional arrangements associated with the economics of aging suggest a careful rethinking of options.

8. Galbraith has focused on the economics of *very large* corporations; there are large numbers of smaller corporations more dependent on external capital markets. However, the flow-of-funds statistics of the Federal Reserve, for example, indicate that funds from internal sources of "nonfarm, nonfinancial corporate businesses" are about 70–80 percent of physical asset purchases.

More Reliance on Individual Decision-Making

It is completely unrealistic to talk about abolishing any or all existing pension programs, and few writers have taken this extreme position. Major shifts in direction, however, may be possible. One such shift would be a move away from our substantial reliance on the increasingly complex collective, compulsory arrangements we have developed to provide economic support in old age. For example, tax subsidies for pension plans could be eliminated or reduced, social security real benefit levels could be frozen, and the Supplemental Security Income program (a variant of a negative income tax scheme) could be expanded to provide a floor based on need.

I think we are unlikely to move in this direction. First there is the very real political resistance from the large numbers of public and private pension supporters. More fundamental, however, is the fact that the option of greater individual reliance rests on the assumptions that (a) workers are willing and able to plan for their old age, and (b) the society is willing to ignore the political pleas of those who do not. The arguments and evidence that cast doubt on the validity of these assumptions have grown over the years and are now voluminous (see, for example, Chapters 4 and 6 of Schulz, 1976b; Chapter 4 of Pechman et al., 1968; James Morgan et al., 1962; Katona, 1964; Morrison, 1974).

Expansion of Private Pensions

Another option is to freeze or reduce the role of social security and expand the role of private pensions. It has been proposed, for example, that we mandate an additional tier of pension coverage along with social security (see Paul, 1972; Sass, 1975). All firms would be required to provide a supplement to the basic social security pension either by (a) maintaining their own private scheme, or by (b) participating in a supplemental government scheme. Benefits and rights under the private schemes would have to equal or exceed those of the supplemental government scheme.

This option, at first glance, may appear to be a rather uncomplicated solution to the pension coverage problem; in the words of Robert D. Paul (1972), "the mechanics of such a system are simple" (see also Sass, 1975). However, actual experience in countries that have gone this route suggests that the truth is just the opposite. French private pensions were mandated and integrated with social security in 1961. The result is a highly complex system of private plans organized under two coordinating and supervisory agencies. To protect workers' pension rights and provide the ability to adjust their pensions for inflation and economic growth, an elaborate pooling arrangement of funds is carried out within the two major systems. Financing is carried out on essentially a pay-as-you-go basis; risks are pooled and the business failure or decline of an individual company is absorbed by the more prosperous ones.

Anyone who has studied the French pension system cannot fail to be impressed by its complexity. More importantly, in order to achieve the key requirements of vesting/portability, security of rights, and inflation protection, the pension structure has been highly centralized and set up very much like a public pension program—so much so that it is difficult to categorize the resulting structure as either private or public.

Great Britain is currently implementing what appears to be a simpler system. This consists of a basic flat-rate social security pension and mandatory supplementary coverage through private pensions or contributions to a governmental earnings-related scheme. This new system is scheduled to begin in 1978, but the government supplemental scheme will not reach full maturity until 20 years after that date.

Members of "contracted out" private pensions and their employers will pay the *full* contribution rate on earnings up to a base level to finance their flat-rate benefits. On earnings between the base level and an upper limit they will pay reduced contributions, in return for certain short-term and disability benefits and partial coverage for earnings-related widows' pensions. The benefits to be paid under the private schemes must be at least as great as those under the government supplemental earnings-related scheme. And, since the government scheme will be based on average earnings revalued upward by an earnings index, private schemes must base their regular and widows' benefits on final earnings or average earnings similarly revalued.

The issue that has caused the most discussion is how to preserve the real value of the vested private benefits of job changers and of private pensions *during* retirement. Under the Labour Government scheme, vested benefits must be maintained so that they are not less, at any point, than the amount under the governmental supplemental scheme for the relevant period of contracted out service. (The latter escalates in line with an earnings index.) Private schemes, however, will be able to limit their liability in this matter to increases no greater than 5 percent per year, by making specified payments to the National Insurance scheme. Protection for increases above 5 percent will then be met by the government through mechanisms yet to be specified. With regard to inflation protection during retirement, the present scheme calls for the government to pay the entire cost of adjusting private pensions for increases in the cost of living. The potential costs and redistributional aspects of these inflation-proofing mechanisms has caused considerable controversy in Britain. Businesses have complained about the anticipated costs of indexing vested benefits, and private pension critics have argued against the further government subsidization of private plans through inflation-proofing (see, for example, Kincaid, 1976).

Raise the Floor of Social Security

Mandating private pension coverage and more detailed specification of private pension standards will no doubt receive increased attention as the actual or projected retirement income gap grows between one-pension and two-pension workers. Pressures from those lacking private pension coverage will no doubt be reenforced by economic and political pressures from the already large and growing private pension industry. Moreover, as Robert Ball (1974) has pointed out, "there is little understanding of who pays for private pension plans, whereas the burden of social security on the worker is visible and, therefore, politically difficult to increase.... It is increasingly difficult for those who have to run for office, whether trade union officials or Congressmen, to support increases in social security contributions, and it is no problem for them to go along with the idea that private pension plans are somehow paid for by employers."

Given these various political and economic pressures toward the expansion of private pensions, a third option may be as unlikely as the first one discussed above. The third option is to expand the role of social security and thereby limit (and in some cases reduce) the role of private pensions. It is this option that I have discussed at some length in a book on social security reform in the United States and abroad (Schulz et al., 1974).

A reasonable retirement goal is *to maintain a living standard in retirement that is not too different from that experienced during a period of years just prior to retirement.*[9] A convenient and useful index of how well pensions contribute toward that goal is the pension replacement rate—the ratio of pension income to defined preretirement earnings.

For vast numbers of workers, the current social security retirement program results in replacement rates below 40 percent of average earnings just prior to retirement (Schulz et al., 1974, Table 49). To maintain living standards in retirement requires replacement rates of

9. Such a goal would not necessarily be satisfactory for those living in poverty or suffering an abnormal drop in income (because of disability, for example) during the designated periods.

about 65 to 75 percent of *gross* preretirement income.[10] Currently, the difference between the social security replacement rate and the 65–75 percent target must be provided by private pensions or individuals' wealth. Raising social security replacement rates narrows this gap.

We have previously proposed that social security replacement rates provide inflation-protected benefits equal to at least 55 percent of an individual's or family's (if married) preretirement average earnings. One measure of preretirement earnings would be to average earnings for the best 10 of the last 15 years prior to retirement (with specified minimum and maximum benefit levels).[11] With this level of replacement achieved in a compulsory, universal, portable, and inflation-protected program, there would be much less reason to worry about how, or whether, the remaining gap is filled.

Certainly there would be less justification for the current trend toward a tier of private pensions subject to a burgeoning variety of government legislation. What we see now is increasing pressure to legislate additional minimum pension standards, to develop elaborate coordinating pension mechanisms, to have the government do a better job of supervisory plans and investigating where problems are indicated, and to develop inflation-proofing techniques (perhaps financed, as in England, in part by the federal government). It is not surprising that many businesses now see the pension fringe benefit as a growing headache, rather than the management tool that was talked about in earlier years.

Even given higher social security replacement rates, some might still argue for mandating an additional level of pension benefits. But it is just as likely that there would be strong support for allowing individual discretion and minimizing government supervision of those private pension plans operating to fill the gap or to satisfy the special retirement objectives of particular industries or occupations.

The current scrutiny and criticism of the social security system by both professionals and the media is helpful, for it is not without faults. But except for the congressional investigations leading up to ERISA, there has been great dearth of professional discussion and analysis of the economic impact and equity of the growing private pension sector.

10. This estimate takes into account reduced expenses in retirement (as estimated by BLS), reduced tax rates, and reduced social security/personal savings contributions.

11. The "best 10 of the last 15" is just one of many possible measures of preretirement earnings that might be used. See Schulz et al. (1974), for a discussion of these various alternatives.

It is important that this imbalance in the pension dialogue and our research efforts not continue. In our future analyses and debates about how to provide economic support in retirement we need to give greater attention to the interaction and combined results of our mixed pension system.

REFERENCES

Ball, Robert (1974). "Social Security and Private Pension Plans," *National Tax Journal* 27 (September): 467–71.

Bernstein, Peter L. (1975). "Capital Shortage: Cyclical or Secular?" *Challenge* (Nov./Dec.), pp. 6–11.

Binstock, Robert H., and Ethel Shanas, eds. (1976). *The Handbook of Aging and the Social Sciences.* New York: Van Nostrand Reinhold.

Boulding, Kenneth (1958). *Principles of Economic Policy.* Englewood Cliffs, N.J.: Prentice-Hall.

Caswell, Jerry (1974). "Economic Efficiency in Pension Plan Administration: A Study of the Construction Industry." Ph.D. dissertation, University of Pennsylvania.

"Current Operating Statistics (1975). *Social Security Bulletin* 38 (July).

Dales, Sophie R. (1974). "Benefits and Beneficiaries under Public Employee Retirement Systems, Calendar Year 1973," Research and Statistics Note No. 21–1974. Washington, D.C.: Social Security Administration.

Equality and Efficiency—The Big Trade-off (1975). Washington, D.C.: Brookings Institution.

"Emerging Issues in Social Legislation" (1967). *Harvard Law Review* 80 (February): 731.

Fox, Alan (1974). *Earnings Replacement from Social Security and Private Pensions: Newly Entitled Beneficiaries, 1970.* Preliminary Findings from the Survey of New Beneficiaries, Report No. 13. Washington, D.C.: Office of Research and Statistics, U.S. Social Security Administration.

Friedman, Barry L., and Leonard J. Hausman (1977). "Welfare in Retreat: A Dilemma for the Federal System," *Public Policy* 25 (Winter): 25–48.

Galbraith, John Kenneth (1967). *The New Industrial State.* New York: New American Library.

Hewitt, Edwin S. (1970). Testimony before the U.S. Senate Special Committee on Aging, *Economics of Aging: Toward a Full Share in Abundance.* Part 10B. Washington, D.C.: Government Printing Office.

Katona, George (1964). *The Mass Consumption Society.* New York: McGraw-Hill.

——— and Burkhard Strumpel (1976). "Consumer Investment Versus Business Investment," *Challenge* (Jan./Feb.), pp. 12–16.

Kincaid, J.C. (1976). "Some Recent Developments in British Pensions," *Industrial Gerontology* 3: 1 (Winter): 41–56.

Kolodrubetz, Walter W. (1974). "Employee-Benefit Plans, 1972," *Social Security Bulletin* 37 (May): 15–21.

____ (1975). "Employee-Benefit Plans, 1973," *Social Security* Bulletin 38 (May): 26.

____ and Donald M. Landay (1973). "Coverage and Vesting of Full-Time Employees under Private Retirement Plans," *Social Security Bulletin* 36 (November): 20–36.

Latimer, Murray (1965). *The Relationship of Employee Hiring Ages to the Cost of Pension Plans* Washington, D.C.: Department of Labor.

Lindsey, Robert (1976). "Pension Plans Cancelled by 5,500 Small Companies," *New York Times*, March 8, pp. 1, 19.

Morgan, James et al. (1962). *Income and Welfare in the United States.* New York: McGraw-Hill.

Morrison, Malcolm (1974). "A Study of the Savings Decisions of Current Workers and their Perceptions of Planning for Income Adequacy in Retirement." Ph.D. dissertation, Brandeis University.

Occupational Pension Schemes (1976). London: Macdermott and Chant Ltd.

Paul, Robert D. (1972). "Pensions: An Issue that Won't Retire," *New York Times*, October 22, Sec. 3, p. 14F.

Pechman, Joseph A., et al. (1968). *Social Security—Perspectives for Reform.* Washington, D.C.: Brookings Institution.

Reports of the Quadrennial Advisory Council on Social Security (1975). House Document No. 94–75. 94th Congress, 1st session. Washington, D.C.: Government Printing Office.

Rimlinger, Gaston (1971). *Welfare Policy and Industrialization in Europe, America and Russia.* New York: Wiley.

"Role of Public and Private Programs in Old-Age Income Assurance" (1968). U.S. Joint Economic Committee, *Old-Age Assurance*, Part I. Washington, D.C.: Government Printing Office.

"The Role of Private Pension Plans in the Economy" (1972). In *Financing Retirement: Public and Private.* Conference Proceedings. New York: Tax Foundation, Inc.

Sass, Sherman G. (1975). "An Actuary's Primer for Social Gerontologists: Policy Issues Involving Private Pension Schemes." Paper presented at the International Congress of Gerontology. Mimeo.

Schiller, Bradley R., and Randall Weiss (1975). "The Impact of Private Pensions on Firm Attachment." Mimeo.

Schulz, James H. (1970). *Pension Aspects of the Economics of Aging: Present and Future Roles of Private Pensions.* Special Senate Committee on Aging, Committee Print. Washington, D.C.: Government Printing Office, pp. 13–16.

____ (1975). "The Need for Age-Neutral Private Pensions," *Industrial Gerontology* 2 (Fall): 255–65.

____ (1976a). "Income Distribution and the Aging," in Robert J. Binstock and Ethel Shanas, eds., *Handbook of Aging and the Social Sciences.* New York: Van Nostrand Reinhold.

____ (1976b). *The Economics of Aging.* Belmont, California: Wadsworth.

____ et al. (1974). *Providing Adequate Retirement Income—Pension Reform in the United States and Abroad.* Hanover, N.H.: New England Press, for Brandeis University Press.

——— and Guy Carrin (1972). "The Role of Saving and Pension Systems in Maintaining Living Standards in Retirement," *Journal of Human Resources* 7 (Summer): 343–65.

Siegfried, Charles A. (1970). "The Role of Private Pensions," in *Private Pensions and the Public Interest.* Washington, D.C.: American Enterprise Institute.

Statistics Canada (1976). *Pension Plans in Canada.* Ottawa: Information Canada.

Subcommittee on Social Security, Committee on Ways and Means (1975). *Financing the Social Security System.* Washington, D.C.: Government Printing Office.

"Tax Expenditures" (1976). U.S. Senate Committee on the Budget. Washington, D.C.: Government Printing Office.

Thurow, Lester C. (1969). "The Optimum Lifetime Distribution of Consumption Expenditures," *American Economic Review* 59 (June): 324–30.

——— (1973). Reply to Daniere critique of "The Optimum Lifetime Distribution . . ." *American Economic Review* 63 (September): 740–55.

——— (1976). "Tax Wealth, Not Income," *New York Times Magazine*, April 11, p. 32.

Tilove, Robert (1976). *Public Employee Pension Funds.* New York: Columbia University Press.

Tracy, Martin B. (1976). "World Developments and Trends in Social Security," *Social Security Bulletin* 39 (April): 14–22.

Trades Union Congress (1976). *Occupational Pension Schemes.* London: Macdermott and Chant Ltd., pp. 11–12.

U.S. Department of Labor (1964). *Labor Mobility and Private Pension Plans*, BLS Bulletin No. 1407. Washington, D.C.: Government Printing Office.

Wallich, Henry C. (1976) "Is There a Capital Shortage?" *Challenge* (Sept./Oct., 1975), pp. 30–43.

Commentary

Comment on Schulz

Robert Tilove

The social security system is obviously entering a time of reformulation. A number of developments have surfaced simultaneously. A mistake in the escalation formula needs to be corrected. Some additional financing is needed for the immediate future. A projected long-range increase in the ratio of beneficiaries to workers requires reexamination of the ultimate financing and occasions questions about the benefit structure. The increasing percentage of women at work will force reexamination of the benefit increment provided for working wives. Increasing payroll taxes stimulate interest in ways of lightening the load on low earners, in measures to contain cost, in ways of shifting the cost of those portions of social security shaped more by social adequacy than "individually earned equity," and in financing from general revenues. Changing times and court decisions stir a need for provisions that will be sex-blind. This symposium is good evidence of the tremendous diversity of choices being urged on the people and the Congress of the United States.

How much should be expected of social security and how much should be expected of private pensions? Professor Schulz makes a valuable contribution when he points out that at least half the workers in the private sector are not covered by pension plans. Those not covered generally earn less than those who are, and they are usually not unionized. The growth of private pension plans in the fifties and sixties was vast, but for several years now it has slowed to a snail's pace. The idea that private plans will by voluntary means

The views expressed in this paper are personal and not necessarily those of Martin E. Segal Company.

come to cover the overwhelming majority of employees is unrealistic. Some people have recently talked about the "individual retirement accounts" established under the Employee Retirement Income Security Act of 1974 as if they will fill the void. In my opinion, that, too, is unrealistic. The kind of person who needs pension coverage the most is the one who can barely make ends meet for current needs, much less think of putting aside $1,500 a year because it is tax deferred.

The situation would be different if there were a layer of private pensions mandated by law, similar to a minimum wage. However, absent that alternative, one cannot validly enter a discussion of what social security should provide in reliance on the facile assumption that practically everybody will also have some private pension or annuity coverage in the foreseeable future. In the absence of much wider coverage by private plans, social security has to be designed adequately to meet the needs of those who have no other pension coverage. While not always acknowledged, the facts are clear and the point is fundamental.

What do we mean by adequate social security? Traditionally, social security has been referred to as the first and basic layer of security for old age and in case of the disability or premature death of the breadwinner. This basic layer might be supplemented by private pensions and by personal savings. Of late, a note has crept into some discussions which refers to the fairly new Supplemental Security Income program as the first and basic layer of protection, with OASDI providing a second layer of more adequate benefits when they have been earned, and after that the private layers.

Both schools start with the view that the government should assume responsibility for eliminating the poverty that so often results when people can no longer work because of age or total disability or they are dependents stranded by the premature death of the wage earner. However, the more traditional school says that the problem should be dealt with by a social insurance system that pays benefits under these categorical circumstances as a matter of earned right. The other school believes that the basic attack on the problem should be through payments based on a means test. I will take my stand with the traditionalists. We think it is better to avoid poverty with plans that grant rights than to measure out a rescue from poverty through any sort of means test. We think of needs programs such as Supplemental Security Income as serving to catch a small minority which cannot be sufficiently encompassed or supported by a social insurance program based upon a substantial history of covered employment.

Professor Schulz suggests that social security might be adequate if it provided replacement of 55 percent of average earnings in the best 10 of the last 15 years preceding eligibility. Whether I would consider that goal reasonable depends to a large extent on how it is defined.

Professor Schulz seems to be thinking of it in terms of the earnings of an individual or a couple, without an additional benefit for a nonworking spouse. I question whether it would be desirable to eliminate a benefit for a nonworking spouse.

Another broad question is the level of earnings to which the 55 percent figure should be applicable. If we are talking about somebody at the low end of the earnings scale who has been a lifelong participant in the labor force, social security already provides at least 55 percent of final earnings if he is married. In the case of a worker who has had median earnings, social security manages to replace about 40 percent of final earnings, and with a spouse, 60 percent. That is at least as good as 55 percent of a ten-year average, considering the fact that the retirees are preponderantly married. The 55 percent figure is not reached, however, for the worker who has earned substantially above average or at the maximum of the social security wage base. I am not sure 55 percent for them should be.

It is no news that social security is heavily tilted in favor of the lower-paid and in favor of married, rather than single, beneficiaries. The social security program has always had to balance "individually earned" equities against the welfare features that serve the demands of social adequacy. In the beginning, both objectives were desirable; in my opinion, they are still desirable. They could stand review and recasting, but they are still desirable.

However, meeting both of these objectives has put great pressure on a mounting payroll tax. These questions, among others, have been raised:

1. Should there be greater emphasis on the individual equities, and therefore less financing of the social adequacy provisions out of the payroll tax?
2. Should the welfare aspects of the social security provisions be shifted to general revenue financing?
3. Should less of social security financing be borne by employee contributions?
4. Should low-wage earners be granted some degree of relief from social security contributions?

On general revenue financing, I must confess I am in the unfortunate position of having sympathies on both sides of the question. An important element, in my judgment, in the historic success of the social security program has been its acceptance as a social insurance program in which rights are earned on the basis of employment and of contributions related to earnings. The social adequacy aspects have not, in my opinion, been disturbing to workers or voters. They understand the idea of adding a benefit for a wife or a widow, and they can understand and appreciate a weighting of the benefit for the lower-paid worker even though it is paid for by the higher-paid worker and that person's employer. The average American may not know the details, but he or she has gotten the idea that it is a good system; it does good things for them; and if there is a certain sharing in favor of the less fortunate, that is not bad.

Another value of this social insurance program of ours is the reliance that people place in it. While Congress has always reserved the right to change the provisions of the law, there has always been fundamental recognition that it has an obligation to fulfill the program's commitments. There is a basic good sense and good faith to the way the program has been handled. We all talk about the need for decoupling the escalation formula; when done, it will probably result in reducing benefits that would otherwise be payable in the year 2000. I do not think that change would disturb anyone. On the other hand, were somebody to suggest that benefits be reduced for people who are going to retire one year hence, Congress would not give it serious consideration. That is as it should be. That compact is made more binding by the fact that it is based on employer and employee contributions. Perhaps that would be equally true if, as in some European systems, the financing were divided on some fixed basis, such as one-third employee, one-third employer, and one-third government.

There has been some uneasiness, however, about the idea of large—but irregular or fluctuating—financing through general revenues. The worry is that what can be made possible through general revenues may also be turned off or diminished by a reduction in general revenues.

On the other hand, there is an excellent case for financing the welfare aspects, even of a social insurance program, out of general revenues. One possibility would be for a particular part of the total program to be clearly defined to be financed out of general revenues. It should be a segment that would be understandable and approvable by the public both as to its benefits and its financing. The idea would be to remove any taint or suspicion of uncertainty.

I would like to vent an idea along these lines, while confessing that I have not yet tried to probe what all of its implications may be. Suppose we recast social security so that it consists of two layers instead of one. The first would be a demogrant of, let us say, $100 per month, granted to everyone upon attainment of a particular age, for example, 65. The $100 would be automatically updated by an indexing formula. The second layer would be strictly related to average indexed earnings in covered employment. It would be a benefit payable in the full amount upon retirement at or after age 65. It might be 25 or 30 percent of average monthly indexed earnings.

There is, of course, nothing very novel about this idea. There are several countries that have two layers in their national programs: the first, a flat pension for everyone, and the second, a graduated social insurance plan.

This sort of change would have many implications. Among the more obvious are these:

1. General revenue would be applied to make payment to every "senior citizen" and part of the payment would come back to the government through taxation on the basis of taxable income.
2. The problem of inequity as between the one-worker couple and the two-worker couple would be eliminated. Each senior citizen would get his or her wage-related benefit plus the $100 a month.
3. The burden on the payroll tax would be lightened or abated.
4. Payable regardless of work after 65, the demogrant would reduce the problem of the post-retirement work test. Of course, to the extent that a beneficiary continued to work, part of the benefit would return to the federal government in the form of taxes.
5. It gives the proper tilt to the combined benefits in favor of the lower-paid worker.
6. It makes an allowance for the spouse who has not been in the labor market.

If you try out this formula, you will see that it comes rather close to reproducing the general results of the social security program. That is not surprising. What this idea does essentially is to take the social adequacy weighting embodied in the social security formula and convert it into a simple demogrant. That applies both to the weighting for the lower-paid and the add-on for wives.

Having made this brief excursion into the broader territory of this conference, I would like to return to the role of private plans. Assume we had an old-age demogrant of $100 a month, indexed, plus a retirement pension of 25 percent of average indexed wages. If that were applied right now, someone earning $15,000 a year would get a combined payment equal to 33 percent replacement, and if his wife had not worked, the replacement would amount to 41 percent when she attained age 65. (Someone with lesser earnings would have a higher replacement ratio because of the flat demogrant.) The 33 percent figure is better than present social security; the 41 percent figure is not as good, except that if the wife had worked enough to qualify for any amount of benefits, they would add to the 41 percent, and as little as 4 percent of her husband's average monthly indexed wage would bring the couple equal to the present law. However, the result for this above-average employee would not make the 55 percent goal, unless the indexed wage was so much higher than the ten-year average.

The question is, How far does the obligation of the government extend? If social need demanded replacement for everyone of 60 or 70 of final average earnings, then we should do it. I am not one to argue that private plans have any God-given right to exist if it is at the expense of social need. On the other hand, there is the serious question whether government should do more than needs doing.

The other part of the question is, What value is there in private provisions, individual or collective? Well, for one, you can have a variety of different decisions. There is no special merit in having one formula, one decision, one consensus, to govern everyone. There is, in fact, a positive value, if you can afford it, in leaving room for individuals and economic organizations—both business and labor—to make their own decisions. They may have particular circumstances to take into account, such as earlier or later retirement, compulsory or voluntary retirement, transitional benefits for second careers in middle years, payments in forms other than life annuities, and so on. Differences may develop even out of varying tastes, preferences, and values. When people do or try things through independent action, they may break out of the mold and create innovations and results that prove useful to themselves and others as well. There is also some value in dispersion of power—power to make decisions, power to control assets, and the like. That all power should reside in the national government, even one that is democratically elected, is by no means an unmixed blessing.

A major argument that has been made in favor of a large private sector is the need for capital investment funds. Of course an adequate rate of investment is necessary for a healthy economy, but it is unclear whether further expansion of social security would dry up necessary sources of capital. There are those who argue that social security, even as it is, has reduced savings in the form of pensions, profit-sharing plans, and personal savings, and has therefore created a shortage of capital investment. I have not seen any convincing evidence of that. On the other hand, would a vast expansion of social security have that effect? I do not know.

There have been difficulties in the past, as Professor Schulz points out, in adequately integrating the provisions of private plans with social security. It is true that integration arrangements (step-rate formulas) have in the past been made obsolete by frequent changes in the social security wage base. It is also true that in the 1950s, offset plans were initially widespread but later eliminated. However, offset plans in one form or another are now enjoying a comeback. The elimination of social security offsets was part of a liberalizing trend at a time when the combination of private benefits and social security was far below preretirement net income. That is no longer universally true, particularly in the case of public employee retirement systems. Therefore, it is not convincing to look at the history of the 1950s and 1960s as disposing of the possibilities of making private pension plans complementary to social security. It can be done, in a variety of ways, and the process is gradually taking place, although as yet to only a relatively slight extent.

Professor Schulz has properly noted the problem of "undershooting" or "overshooting" retirement income goals if social security is fixed by the national government while half the workers in private industry have no pension coverage and the other half do, by decisions made elsewhere than in Congress. One part of the problem—perhaps not the major part, but at least substantial—is that many public employee retirement plans are already fixed at a level such that with any substantial increase in social security, overshooting will be a common phenomena at public expense. Moreover, these are plans the benefits of which cannot, as a legal, moral, or practical matter, be diminished for persons already employed.

The idea of a mandatory layer of pensions has been advanced in an effort to reduce the gap between the half presently without coverage and the half now enjoying private plan coverage. The idea is for legislation to require every employer to set up a pension plan meeting certain minimum specifications. To employers meeting those requirements or exceeding them by virtue of their present plans, this would be no additional burden. To all others, it would involve additional cost. It would seem desirable to consider the program in the simplest possible terms, such as, for example, a contribution for each employee equal to *X* percent of pay, accumulated with an interest credit, fully vested, and convertible at the appropriate retirement age into an annuity. There could be a supplemental government annuity fund for handling these accounts or the employer could contract out to a private arrangement.

Professor Schulz has pointed out that countries with this sort of a contracting-out arrangement have had difficulties, including undue complexities and the problem of how to escalate—for cost-of-living or wage changes—benefit amounts that were accrued with some earlier employer. Perhaps we in the United States would not get quite as complicated. This idea is not to take away or split off any part of our social security benefits, and they are substantial and indexed. Consequently, there would seem to be less need in our case for insisting on the updating of benefits, with all the difficulties it would entail. After all, the private pension plans that we now have do not attempt to escalate benefits for the cost of living, much less for wage changes after retirement. If a mandated layer is a substantial step toward matching existing pensions, then it will have served to alleviate the gap between the covered and the uncovered.

Mandated supplemental pensions through a simple, fully vested, fully re-insured, money-purchase plan is not the ideal design for adequate income in retirement, and particularly not for the near future, because the accumulations take time to build up. However, if we can maintain an adequate social security system, such a layer may prove to be a valuable supplement, both to savings for investment and for greater equity throughout our economy in terms of retirement income.

Social security should be the basic layer of protection. It should provide benefits as a matter of right adequate to assure avoidance of poverty for the relatively low-paid worker who has been persistently part of the labor market. The benefits should be tapered to replacement ratios for those with higher earnings that are lower but nevertheless adequately rewarding for the greater contributions. On this basis, social security will fulfill its socially necessary function and considerable room will remain for supplementation by pension plans and personal savings.

 *Chapter 2*

Income, Economic Status, and Policy Toward the Aged

Marilyn Moon
Eugene Smolensky

I

Being old is a condition we all hope to attain, hence everyone can see some personal advantage in social policy which assists the aged. The tension between providing aid and simultaneously discouraging work effort appears to trouble policy-makers less when the elderly are involved than with the other disproportionately poor groups. In addition, the aged comprise a large and savvy lobby. For these reasons the aged are especially favored by public policy. In 1972, for example, transfers "lifted almost half of those who would have been poor in the absence of transfers over the poverty line, but . . . two-thirds of the aged who were poor were lifted out of income poverty" (Lampman, 1976, p. 9).

Yet there remain unexploited options, some relatively inexpensive, which would improve the welfare of many aged. Most of these options have received little public discussion but we suspect they would command wide acceptance. We believe that one explanation for this lack of discussion lies in a technical matter. The conceptions of economic well-being in general and poverty in particular have been unduly constrained because they have been defined in strictly money income terms. Policy-makers use money income not because

This paper was supported by the Administration on Aging and funds granted to the Institute for Research on Poverty at the University of Wisconsin–Madison by the Department of Health, Education, and Welfare pursuant to the Economic Opportunity Act of 1964. Thanks for comments on an earlier draft are owed to Michael Barth, Sheldon Danziger, Irwin Garfinkel, Robert Lampman and Jennifer Warlick. The opinions expressed are those of the authors.

it is a good measure, but because it is an easy one to implement. As a consequence our public policy targets for the aged also become defined in money income terms. More importantly, the emphasis on money income leads to unsatisfactory policy in four ways:

1. Equals are not always treated equally.
2. Unequals are sometimes treated as equals.
3. Minimum levels of potential consumption for aged families are not reached by many who could attain it with a different allocation of the same level of expenditures.
4. Desirable policy alternatives are obscured, when measures and targets are inappropriately specified.

Just as the money income definition causes us to overlook some options, an alternative, albeit improved, measure of economic welfare may also be misleading in some instances. Consequently, the policy proposals we raise here are not meant to be firm recommendations, but rather suggestions for further study. Since assuring horizontal and vertical equity is an important policy goal, the development of new programs needs to be examined from many vantage points to insure that we do not merely replace old inequities with new ones.

In what follows we first indicate in general terms what we think an appropriate measure of well-being should be. In Section III we take up specific additions to money income which would improve that measure. In each instance we (1) briefly present problems of imputing these additions, and (2) discuss problems with current policies and possible solutions consistent with the expanded measure of well-being. In several cases it would be inappropriate to add a particular element of well-being to a measure unless a particular policy was also introduced. Unless the component is attainable by aged families, its inclusion would also mis-state economic welfare. In Section IV, we discuss issues of horizontal and vertical equity across age groups since concentration on programs aimed only at the elderly can lead to inequities of another sort. A brief conclusion terminates the paper.

II

Measuring Economic Well-Being

Indexes of economic welfare ought to capture a family's command over all goods and services: it should measure neither actual levels of consumption nor actual levels of income, but rather the resource constraint faced by the family. Attainable rather than attained consumption is what it is appropriate to measure. By this criterion the traditional money income measure is obviously inadequate. It ignores or understates many resources available to the aged. Net worth, eligibility for in-kind transfers, the amount of leisure time taken, and living arrangements are among the determinants of consumption possibilities inadequately captured in money income. In addition, year-to-year fluctuations in total income cast serious doubt on the use of money income in any one year as the appropriate measure of economic welfare. Permanent income or life-cycle measures smooth out these fluctuations, yielding a more reasonable estimate of what a family could consume in any one year.[1] Incorporating net worth and human capital (expected future earnings) into an economic status measure establishes such a life-cycle measure. Families at the same current income level may, therefore, vary substantially in their capacity to command goods and services. Money income as an indicator of economic status cannot guarantee the identification of "equals." Furthermore, including these nonincome components in a measure of economic status can change the rank ordering of families; attempts to achieve the appropriately unequal treatment of unequals may be misdirected by focusing on current income.

III

Capital

Net Worth. Property income in part reflects the amount of net worth owned by a family. However, asset ownership adds more to economic welfare than is indicated by property income. Some of net worth generates no money income. Moreover, the optimal allocation of that equity over the remaining lifetime of an individual can add significantly to potential consumption in any period while being apportioned so as not to "prematurely" draw down the value of net worth. Thus, an annuitized portion of net worth which effectively incorporates property income can more comprehensively measure the contribution of this economic welfare component (Weisbrod and Hansen, 1968).

For example, consider home equity, the largest component of the assets of the aged, and the least liquid. Home ownership produces no income, yet the home generates a yield, "imputed rent," which is equal at least to the money income yielded by other assets, such as savings and loan shares. One aged family identical to another in every other respect except that it owned and occupied a $15,000 house while the other held $15,000 in a savings account would appear to

1. See, for example, Ando and Modigliani (1963) or Friedman (1957).

some to be at a disadvantage (its money income is less), but to others to have an advantage (its monthly out-of-pocket consumption expenditures would be less). Yet the two are likely to be quite similar in economic well-being properly measured. Obviously the implicit rent from owner-occupied housing belongs in a measure of economic well-being if we are to achieve vertical and horizontal equity.

Some have gone further and suggested that the annuitized value of the house (and all other assets) should be added to current income. When an annuitized value of net worth is substituted for property income in measures of well-being, both the absolute level of measured well-being and the rankings of aged families are altered substantially (Moon, forthcoming). However, given current capital market institutions, the inclusion of a flow equivalent of net worth in a measure of economic well-being is misleading. Consuming out of the net worth of a house implies a smooth reduction of housing services over time. Moreover, such an amount would exceed the value of imputed rent in the normal case where the owner's life expectancy is shorter than the expected "life" of the home.[2] Transaction costs currently make this quite impractical. Consequently, various "actuarial mortgage plans" which would permit the aged to transfer ownership to some

2. Traditionally, home equity is measured as the capitalized value of the total flow of housing services (rental services). The value of the home to the aged owner can be further subdivided into the value of the housing services the homeowner receives during his or her lifetime and the "salable" value of the home when the owner dies. This latter portion consists of the capitalized value of services from the death of the owner, for the remaining life of the house:

$$H = \sum_{t=t_0}^{n} \frac{R_t}{(1+v)^t} + \sum_{t=n}^{D} \frac{R_t}{(1+v)^t}$$

where:

H = value of home to the owner

t_0 = the present time

n = years of life expectancy of the aged person (or surviving spouse, whichever is longer)

R_t = rental value of services in period t

D = expected life of the home in years

v = rate of time preference.

The first term represents a lifetime in-kind housing annuity. The second portion could hypothetically be sold to, say, an insurance company in exchange for a lifetime cash annuity. The aged person (and spouse) would reside in the house rent-free until the death of the surviving member, at which time the insurance company would receive title to the property.

intermediary while retaining rent-free residence for life have been proposed to deal with this problem.[3] Apart from changes in the tax code, some role for government in insuring the state of the property would probably be required. The result would be to allow the home-owner to add to current consumption some amount greater than the imputed rent. Specifically, the owner could also benefit from some portion of the flow of rental services that would remain after the owner's death. In 1969 just over 70 percent of all aged families, including some of the aged poor, owned their own homes (Chen, 1971, pp. 21–22). Thus, given the potential for improving the well-being of the aged from such an institutional change, such proposals deserve serious study.

However, until such an institution exists, it is inappropriate to include the full value of annuitized net worth in any measure of well-being. Further, until such arrangements are feasible, pressure to make second-best adjustments for house ownership but which violate horizontal equity are likely to prove irresistable. "Circuit-breaker" rules, for example, which limit property tax payments by aged property owners but not others with the same income, represent a frequent response to the illiquidity of homes in the portfolios of the aged (Bendick, 1974). Others have suggested that the aged should be allowed to defer property tax payments entirely until the home is sold or the owner dies. Such proposals would implicitly raise the current "liquid" resource level, and hence command over goods and services, for aged homeowners. Thus, they do raise potential consumption for his group while creating some equity problems.

Human Capital and the Value of Leisure. Expected future earnings are an important component of the present value of a lifetime resource constraint. For any one period, current earnings may provide little information about the future level of earned income. Families with large amounts of human capital (the capitalized value of expected future earnings) can expect to draw upon that source in the future and consequently can consume more today out of current income and, in some cases, can even borrow against future expected earned income. In general, younger families have more human capital and hence higher expected future incomes. Net worth holdings become increasingly important the older the family. Nonetheless, any measure which includes only a net worth adjustment or only a human capital adjustment will have a bias which is particularly acute across age groups. Public policy, however, does much to discourage

3. For a specific example of such an actuarial mortgage plan, see Chen (1967).

work by the aged, and hence reduces future earnings and prematurely lowers human capital.

While much attention is centered on maintaining work incentives among the general population, the opposite occurs for the aged. The Supplemental Security Income program, as well as other public assistance, contains a stiff implicit tax rate on earnings (and all other sources of income). Even more important, the much larger social security retirement program alters the labor-leisure choice for many aged households. Taussig (1975), for example, constructs an example in which the earnings of an aged couple eligible for both social security and SSI is taxed at a 0.96 marginal rate. Social security now allows an individual to keep up to the first $2,760 in earnings with no reductions. Then, a 50 percent implicit tax rate is levied against any additional earnings. When combined with the appropriate income tax rate, this 50 percent social security tax on earnings is one of the highest rates any employed person in the United States can face, and undoubtedly discourages work effort. In particular, those who would earn between $2,760 and roughly $9,500 will tend to consume more leisure than otherwise, reflecting the distortion from the earnings tax.[4] Moreover, it particularly discourages those who have the least flexibility in terms of hours worked. When combined with mandatory retirement at age 65 in some industries, many able-bodied workers may be completely excluded from the labor force.

Of course, the aged often voluntarily retire or choose to work shorter hours even in the absence of government incentives. Moreover, since leisure is a normal good, leisure time should also enter the family's measured economic welfare. The presence of government incentives, however, lowers the opportunity cost of leisure below the wage rate and complicates its valuation. Undoubtedly the resulting net effect for many families is a reduction in total economic well-being. Even though the decrease in labor-force participation is just offset by an increase in leisure hours, the valuation of the time differs in the two uses. Thus, the problems in measuring both human capital and leisure time result from the work disincentives directed at the aged.

One policy approach is to reduce these distortions on the labor-leisure choice due to social security. The earnings limit on social security, removed now at 72, could be removed earlier, or the implicit tax made less steep, or the set-aside raised. If the limit on allowed

4. At earning levels above $2,760, social security benefits are reduced by 50 cents for every additional dollar earned. For the average aged worker (who works throughout the year) with one dependent, benefits will be exhausted at about $9,500, which is twice the average benefit received plus $2,760.

earnings provision were removed for everyone over, say, 65, there obviously would be one less work disincentive. A lower implicit tax would make leisure less attractive but still distort choices for some individuals. Finally, if the level of allowed earnings, and hence the range of income subject to the tax, were to increase substantially, many aged workers would escape the distorting effects on the labor-vs.-leisure decision. Certainly a substantive change in the earnings test cannot be practically accomplished while holding all other aspects of social security unchanged; the costs would be substantial. However, a more appropriate policy should mitigate the drastic reduction in earnings that occurs when able-bodied workers are discouraged from remaining in the labor force past age 65. In particular, leaving the transfer levels as they are and hence the work disincentive effects as they are, but lowering the implicit marginal tax rate on benefits toward the marginal tax rate on earnings, would reduce the undesirable substitution effects inherent in the current system.[5] For those relatively few who would return to the labor force because of a change in social security we can expect an increase in real and in measured economic well-being.

A second possible policy change would affect mandatory retirement. If firms were not allowed to force individuals to retire at age 65, more individuals would be able to remain in the labor force. Even though there are at present no universal mandatory retirement provisions, an individual forced to leave one job will find it difficult to achieve employment elsewhere. Protection of the Civil Rights Act of 1964 could be extended beyond age 65 for individuals willing and able to remain active. The result of such policy changes would be to appropriately increase the value of human capital in an expanded measure of economic status for those families whose choices would differ when the incentive structure changed.

Finally, federal income tax provisions for the aged specifically allow the exemption of transfer income, such as social security and SSI payments, and some property income (via the Retirement Income Tax Credit). No such preferential treatment is available for earned income except insofar as the aged benefit from other exemptions or exclusions.[6] Thus, the tax benefits made available to elderly

5. Since leisure is a marginal good, that is, more of it is desired at higher income levels, *ceteris paribus*, earnings are less desirable when an alternative source of income becomes available (the income effect). The substitution effect arises from the rise in the value of leisure time at the margin relative to the wages. The relative price change results in turn because earnings are taxed while leisure is not.

6. However, improvements or changes in these tax subsidies are more likely to affect wealthier aged families.

families may provide incentive for substituting transfers or pensions for earned income.

All of these proposals would encourage more individuals to remain in the labor force past age 65. Such policy would reduce the sharp decline in incomes among those who desire and are able to continue working. Part of the discrepancy in the contribution of earnings to well-being between aged and younger families has been encouraged by policies that coerce older workers to leave the labor force prematurely. Certainly that has historically been the direct intention of many such policies. However, the future decline in the rate of growth in the labor force may change attitudes. From the standpoint of facilitating increases in the level of economic welfare for the aged, it is desirable to reduce the barriers and incentive structure that discourage the able-bodied aged who want to work. Moreover, such changes could lead to a reduction in government transfers to the aged with no decline in well-being for this group. Obviously, providing protection against discrimination should increase employment and decrease some transfers. In addition the costs from a change in the work disincentive from earnings limits on social security could eventually be partially offset by a decline in total transfers. Other income-tested transfers such as Supplemental Security Income and Medicaid may fall when the aged are able to both work and retain some social security.

Intrafamily Transfers

Another important aspect of economic welfare, only partially included in measured money income, is aid from relatives. Cash gifts from relatives outside the nuclear family are included in measures of current income, although these may be underreported. In-kind transfers from outside the family are not captured. But even more important is *intrafamily* aid, often in the form of an in-kind transfer. Intrafamily transfers occur when two or more nuclear families reside together in an extended family group, thus sharing resources. Particularly among certain portions of the population—for example, the young or old—such living arrangements may have an important bearing on the level of economic welfare.

While these living arrangements are undertaken for a wide range of motives, economic incentives must count among the most important. In general, "doubling-up" is a less costly way to provide for needy relatives than through cash transfers or other means. Most people disapprove of such living arrangements and bring relatives into the family only to provide support. About three-fourths of dependent "extra adult units" improve their economic situation by living with relatives, while only 5 percent of those units are worse off than if they lived alone (Morgan et al., 1962). Approximately one-fourth of all aged families resided in extended units and had potential transfers. These aged families can be either donors or recipients of the transfers. In 1967 the aged were about equally divided between the two and were able to provide or receive an average of $1,990.[7] Families within which transfers may be taking place tend to be at the extremes of the income and economic welfare distributions.

Some government programs discourage such resource sharing. Simply making public transfers available has an income effect which discourages intrafamily transfers toward the public transfer recipients. In most cases, however, intrafamily transfers reduce income-tested public transfer payments dollar for dollar. Consequently, intrafamily transfers help needy aged families only if the donors provide greater aggregate support than does the battery of income-tested programs open to the aged. That is, only if the transfer would be greater than the income-tested payments will the aged benefit. When the aged and their children are both relatively poor and would benefit most from doubling up, the incentives against it are greatest. This substitution effect could be mitigated by a more reasonable marginal tax rate.

The recently enacted Supplemental Security Income program provides a particularly severe disincentive. To reflect the provision of room and board, the recipient's benefit is automatically reduced by one-third if the aged reside with relatives. This tax, which is proportional to SSI benefits but is unrelated to the actual intrafamily transfers, may therefore be equivalent to a 100 percent tax rate or more on the intrafamily transfer. This reduction can be avoided only if the potential recipient can establish that he or she received no aid or paid an equal share of all household expenses. The burden of proof falls on the recipients. Unless the savings from residing together equal at least the full amount of payments lost, the economic incentives are for the aged to live apart from relatives. An aged individual who receives only partial support from relatives can suffer a decline in total economic welfare. If intrafamily sharing is not to be discouraged, the implicit tax rate on the benefits of living together should be considerably less than 100 percent.

Another disincentive for families to live in "extended" units and share expenses and duties arises from the federal personal income tax. In many instances, child-care expenditures may be deducted from income, but never when relatives care for the children. Thus, if

7. These calculations from Moon (forthcoming) represent estimates of potential rather than actual transfers.

an aged relative received support partially as a *quid pro quo* for providing child-care services, this amount is not deductible (nor, however, is the aid received taxed). Although in certain circumstances the family may be able to claim the aged person as a dependent, and hence take a $750 personal exemption, this amount may not reflect the full payment, explicit or implicit, to the elderly relative.

Income-tested government programs and the federal personal income tax discourage the sharing of resources among relatives. Lower levels of well-being among some of the aged poor is the probable result.[8] Moreover, the negative incentives for doubling up probably contribute to the trend toward increased responsibility on government to provide transfers to this population group. This then is an area where less stringent provisions might lead to increased well-being on the part of the aged, particularly the poor, and, over time, to greater participation by relatives in achieving such improvements.

In-Kind Transfers and Tax Subsidies

Another component of economic welfare only partially captured by current income is the direct contribution of government. Most current income measures include the value of cash transfer payments, and after-tax income has frequently been cited as an indicator of economic status. In-kind transfers and taxes other than income and payroll taxes, however, are not commensurable with money income and are frequently ignored. The effects of tax subsidies, which alter income tax liability differentially among the aged, are also often overlooked.

One definition of in-kind transfers is the difference between what a taxpayer would voluntarily pay for a good or service and what it actually costs. By this criterion every program includes some transfer, and the distribution of the benefits and burdens of all taxes and expenditures by income class has been frequently calculated (Reynolds and Smolensky, 1974). In-kind transfers are more usually considered to be those goods and services provided by government to clearly assigned beneficiaries at less than marginal cost. Medicare, Medicaid, food stamps, and public housing are the most important in-kind programs to the aged. These programs pose a difficult valua-

8. If fortiutous circumstances like the income or benevolence of ones offspring was the primary determinant of intrafamily transfers, then including these transfers dollar-for-dollar when calculating benefit eligibility would be appropriate when determining who are equals. If, however, benefit levels primarily determine the size of intrafamily transfers, then it is inappropriate to include these transfers as defining equals for programatic purposes. Which of these alternatives is typical is an empirical question. Our guess is that the recent rapid rise in transfer levels now makes the current treatment regressive.

tion problem since most economists expect the recipient of in-kind transfers to value them at some unknown amount less than their cost (Smolensky et al., 1974). Essentially this results from the fact that cash provides greater options: if recipients have the cash, they can buy medical services in the same amount as Medicare provides. Alternatively, with that cash they can buy somewhat less medical care and a lot more booze, and be still happier, if that better satisfies their tastes. Even valued at their cash equivalence to the recipients, however, in-kind transfers probably constitute a significant portion of the economic resources of the aged (Smolensky et al., 1974).

An expanded measure of economic status incorporating in-kind transfers would better identify the poor. Both absolute living levels and the ranking of families will change as compared to money income. However, a new poverty threshold—the cut-off level which distinguishes the poor from the nonpoor—would be required, since these transfers are provided in the form of services or goods. The official poverty lines use current income to establish poverty thresholds. The threshold is derived by estimating a subsistence annual food budget for various family sizes and compositions and then multiplying by a factor representing the share of income a poor family tends to spend on food.[9] For several reasons this indicator is inappropriate for use with a nonincome measure of economic status. For example, the budgets obviously make no allowance for medical care. Implicitly they assume that medical care would be obtained through public assistance, public hospitals, or private charity. Consequently it would be inappropriate to have families classified above the poverty line because an in-kind medical transfer is added to money income. Medicare and Medicaid merely substitute for, though they may augment, previously provided public services not included in the poverty threshold.

Consider the alternative. Public programs provided $673 in per capita medical benefits in 1973, which equaled 23 percent of the 1973 Social Security Administration's poverty threshold for an aged couple (Cooper and Piro, 1974). While the value of medical benefits might technically bring families above the poverty line, they would still be unable to purchase other necessities, since health benefits are given in-kind. Moreover, even those in-kind services that provide goods or services included in the poverty budget, such as public housing, may create problems. If a housing benefit exceeds the amount allowed in the budget, it may also bring above the poverty line families who are unable to acquire subsistence levels of other necessities.

9. See, for example, Orshansky (1968).

At the least, a measure of the needs of an aged family should be as comprehensive as the expanded measure of economic status to which it is applied.

Thus, while in-kind programs surely help to raise a substantial number of families out of poverty, their contribution may be overstated. Benefits to recipients are likely to be less than their cost. Moreover, since they are granted in-kind, they may provide a greater than subsistence amount of that one commodity to the aged, but that good may not substitute for other necessities. For example, the empirical results from a study by Moon (forthcoming) would indicate that in-kind transfers "reduced" the number of families in poverty, using the SSA threshold, by 31 percent in 1967. These transfers were not adjusted for either recipient valuation or the imbalance problems described above, and hence undoubtedly overstate the amount of actual poverty reduction. Similarly, Smeeding (forthcoming) calculates a 54.7 percent reduction in poverty for 1972 after adjusting for recipient-valued in-kind transfers, the underreporting of cash transfers, and tax incidence. Again, his figures may overstate the reduction. Thus, we should be careful in automatically reducing cash or other in-kind transfers in response to the apparent poverty reduction from one in-kind program. While we may have solved a special problem, such as the need for medical care, the problem of poverty may remain.

Tax subsidies or expenditures are those features of the tax code which reduce tax receipts from what they would be in the "ordinary" case. Tax expenditures important to the aged are the failure to tax implicit rent, the double personal exemption, the exemption of interest on state and local bonds, the Retirement Income Tax Credit, and the exclusion of both cash and in-kind transfers (private as well as public) from adjusted gross income. Because of the large number of these programs, and because they usually take the form of a deduction rather than a credit (not to mention a refundable credit), any one program is redundant for all but a minority of the high-income elderly. For example, in 1975 an aged couple would pay no tax until it received an income 1.79 times as large as the appropriate poverty threshold (Danziger and Kesselman, 1975, p. 34). For measurement purposes, this implies that valuation of the benefits from each program for each household requires information on all the programs affecting each aged person. From the policy perspective, vertical equity might be improved if these varying programs were merged into a simple refundable tax credit formula whose distributional impact would be known with some degree of accuracy, *ex ante*. Tax expenditures accrue primarily to recipients of property income and from public and private transfers. If the purpose of the programs is to raise current resources of the aged by reducing tax liabilities, those aged whose main income source is wages are subject to horizontal inequity.

IV

Equal Treatment of Equals

Thus far we have discussed proposals designed to improve the degree of horizontal and vertical equity among the aged. Equity questions across age groups have been ignored. To single out any one demographic group for policy consideration implicitly adds an additional dimension to the definition of equity. For example, in an effort to improve policy for the aged, we could attempt to guarantee two individuals aged 65 and 70, who have equal command over goods and services, equitable tax or transfer treatment. However, if an individual of age 60 also has an initial command over goods and services equal to that of one aged 65, but is denied access to a particular program, we are implicitly using age as an additional criterion for horizontal equity. Although the aged have long been subject to preferential treatment, this policy ought to be reexamined. As an equity criterion age is certainly subject to misuse and may actually be judged discriminatory.

One argument used to support preferential treatment for the elderly is that age—as opposed to, say, race—is a more reasonable criterion. It reflects part of the life cycle to which all individuals are subject. Moreover, to the extent that current income is the determinant of program eligibility it may be argued that the measure has a different meaning for the aged than for younger families. In particular the current income of the aged may be closer to permanent income, on average. However, the expanded measures of economic welfare advocated here capture additional sources of command over goods and services, such as human capital, that vary across age groups. Moreover, some of these measures even seek to reflect the permanent or life-cycle resource level for this group. Hence, if the well-being of all families could be estimated by such measures, the rationale for differential treatment for the aged would be weakened. A life-cycle approach eliminates age bias in the measurement of economic welfare. Moreover, if the policy changes advocated here were implemented, the aged would better be able to utilize various resources. Consequently, unless other claims can be made for preferential treatment of aged families, horizontal and vertical equity should not be complicated by categorization. Redistributional programs to aid the aged poor then would be the same as for other poor families.

Specifically, this could result in changes in Supplemental Security Income which tends to be more generous and less restrictive than Aid to Families with Dependent Children. Conversely, cash programs to younger families could be upgraded to match SSI. This in turn could alter participation in Medicaid and Food Stamps which are often closely related to eligibility for cash programs. On the tax side, preferential treatment from tax expenditures such as the double personal exemption and Retirement Income Tax Credit could no longer be readily justified for the aged alone. Also, programs to ease the burden of the property tax for low income aged families would have to be justified as beneficial for all the poor or for reasons other than redistribution. Thus, some programs that currently benefit only the aged could be extended to all families or be eliminated thereby satisfying horizontal and vertical equity. The retention of such programs in their present form would have to be justified on some other basis.

If economic status were appropriately measured, and if institutions for the orderly liquidation (or accumulation) of wealth were in place, and if we were as concerned about creating disincentives to work among the aged as we are for others, and if smoothing out one source of earnings variability were as socially relevant as smoothing out any other source producing equal variability, then age would lose its special place in the income-maintenance system and horizontal equity could be vastly improved. Until the millenium, however, policy proposals for the aged will, in most cases, create horizontal inequities across age classes.

V

CONCLUSION

Over the past decade, concern with the design and evaluation of antipoverty programs has led to a critical review of existing indexes of economic welfare and to the development of alternatives. The starting point has invariably been "cash income," that is, income plus cash transfers. However, for some families current cash receipts represent only a small portion of the available sources of economic welfare. Differing amounts of voluntarily chosen leisure time, in-kind transfers, physical and human capital, and special tax treatment can substantially alter the economic position of families with similar cash incomes. For this reason other sources of purchasing power are often added to create alternative indexes of family status. These are central if we intend to provide similar treatment to families at equivalent levels of economic status. For example, government programs directed at poor families often intend to include all those who are poor and to exclude totally those who are not poor. When receipt or denial of substantial benefits turns on an empirical index, it is obviously important for that index to conform to a generally shared view of both horizontal and vertical equity. More comprehensive measures of economic status which better distinguish poor from nonpoor families increase the likelihood of policy improvements that will treat equally those who society views as equals.

More important than any improvement in measurement are the policy implications a broader conception of economic status suggests. Before these augmented measures of economic status can be used to evaluate the distributional effects of tax and transfer programs, the measures' components must be attainable by aged families. We have suggested four areas of possible policy changes. Illiquid assets could presumably provide a substantial flow of current purchasing power to the aged. Use of this largely untapped source could be encouraged by the government at relatively little expense. The second and third areas imply a reduction in disincentives resulting from the substitution effects elicited by current policy toward the aged. Labor-force participation and more efficient living arrangements, which could both increase the well-being of elderly families, are now discouraged. Policy to reduce these disincentives may be costly. Finally, the net contribution of government to well-being requires a proper accounting of the benefits. Inclusion of in-kind transfers should be used in a measure that establishes eligibility for transfer programs. However, we must not overstate these benefits and hence unfairly reduce payments from other programs. Moreover, when taxes are appropriately measured, the redundancy of tax subsidies for the aged poor become apparent, suggesting a need for change. It is important to point out that while these policy changes should all affect the aged poor, they are directed at treating all aged families fairly. Moreover, as is suggested in the last section, concern for horizontal and vertical equity leads us to question the use of any category, such as age, in establishing eligibility for government aid if income is properly defined.

REFERENCES

Ando, Albert, and Franco Modigliani (1963). "The 'Life Cycle' Hypothesis of Saving: Aggregate Implications and Tests," *American Economic Review* 53 (March): 55–84.

Bendick, Mark (1974). "Designing Circuit Breaker Property Tax Relief," *National Tax Journal* 27 (March): 19–28.

Chen, Yung-Ping, (1971). *Income*. 1971 White House Conference on Aging. Washington, D.C.: Government Printing Office.

_____ (1967). "Potential Income from Homeownership: An Actuarial Mortgage Plan," in *Old Age Income Assurance*, Part II, Joint Economic Committee. Washington, D.C.: Government Printing Office.

Cooper, Barbara S., and Paula A. Piro (1974). "Age Differences in Medical Care Spending, Fiscal Year 1973," *Social Security Bulletin* (May): 3–14.

Danziger, Sheldon, and Johnathan R. Kesselman, (1975). "Personal Exemptions and Per Capita Credits in the U.S. Income Tax." Discussion Paper #271. Institute for Research on Poverty, Madison, Wisconsin.

Friedman, Milton (1957). *A Theory of the Consumption Function.* New York: National Bureau of Economic Research, Inc.

Lampman, Robert (1976). "Economics of Social Welfare." Mimeo.

Moon, Marilyn (forthcoming). "The Economic Welfare of the Aged and Income Security Programs," *Review of Income and Wealth.*

Morgan, James, et al. (1962). *Income and Welfare in the United States.* New York: McGraw-Hill.

Orshansky, Mollie (1968). "The Shape of Poverty in 1966," *Social Security Bulletin* (March), pp. 3–31.

Reynolds, Morgan, and Eugene Smolensky (1974). "The Post Fisc Distribution: 1961 and 1970 Compared," *National Tax Journal* 27 (December): 515–30.

Smeeding, Timothy (forthcoming). "The Economic Well-Being of Low Income Households: Implications for Income Inequality and Poverty," in Marilyn Moon and Eugene Smolensky, eds., *Improving Economic Measures of Well-Being.* New York: Academic Press.

Smolensky, Eugene, et al. (forthcoming). "Adding In-kind Transfers to the Personal Income and Outlay Account: Implications for the Size Distribution of Income." Conference on Income and Wealth.

Taussig, Michael K. (1975). "The Social Security Retirement Program and Welfare Reform," in Irene Lurie, ed., *Integrating Income Maintenance Programs*, New York: Academic Press.

Weisbrod, Burton A., and W. Lee Hansen (1968). "An Income–Net Worth Approach to Measuring Economic Welfare," *American Economic Review* 58 (December): 1315–29.

Commentary

Comment on Moon and Smolensky

Robin Jane Walther

In the past decade, the quantitative assessment of the economic well-being of the older population as well as other population groups has received considerable attention. Most work in this area has been based on the assumption that money income is an inadequate measure of economic well-being in that benefits derived from asset ownership, from leisure, and from private and public nonmonetary transfers are excluded. Various techniques have been suggested for augmenting the measure of simple money income to a more comprehensive measure of economic well-being (Morgan, 1965; Taussig, 1973; Moon, 1975).

The preceding paper by Moon and Smolensky provides us both with a description of an additional measure of economic status and with some suggestions about the possible uses of this measure in the formulation and evaluation of social policies. The measure of economic status they describe is relatively comprehensive, including adjustments of money income for asset ownership, leisure time and human capital, and private and public transfers. Notable for their absence are discussions of the adjustment of money income for the health of the individual and for the uncertainty attached to future incomes. Although the specific policy proposals for the reform of income maintenance and employment programs are not particularly original, these proposals do suggest some possible uses for the measures of economic status which are currently being developed.

The research for this paper was supported by the Administration on Aging Grant No. 90–A–643/01.

Here, the measure of economic well-being suggested by Moon and Smolensky is considered. Comments about their numerous policy proposals are restricted to those policies directly related to the use of chronological age.

MEASURING ECONOMIC WELL-BEING

Before any empirical measure of economic well-being is developed, the reason for developing the measure needs to be established. Ideally, the reason for developing the measure will determine the appropriate theoretical definition of economic well-being, and this theoretical definition will guide the empirical specification of the measure. Without a carefully specified theoretical definition of economic well-being, the extent to which the empirical measure approximates the theoretical measure cannot be determined.

Measures of economic well-being have generally been developed in order to evaluate and design equitable social policies. In order to translate this reason for developing a measure of economic well-being into a theoretical definition of economic well-being, the basic criterion to be used in defining an equitable distribution needs to be established. If an endowment-based criterion is adopted, then the appropriate definition of economic well-being is an objective measure in which the value assigned family resources is determined by a market price. If a utilitarian or economic welfare criterion is adopted, the appropriate definition of economic well-being is a subjective measure in which the value assigned resources is dependent on individual preferences.

Additional issues regarding the theoretical definition of economic well-being include specification of the appropriate time period and definition of the family unit. The choice of a specific definition is largely determined by the primary purpose for developing the measure. For example, if the purpose for developing the measure is to assess the extent to which attainable consumption differs among aged family units, the time period will be specified as the remaining life of the aged unit and the family as either a married couple or a single person.

Once the reasons for developing a measure of economic well-being and the theoretical definition of economic well-being are established, the specific data set to be used for the empirical work can be selected. The actual empirical specification of economic well-being will be guided both by the theoretical definition and by the type of information contained in the specific data source. Each empirical measure should be judged by the extent to which it efficiently uses the available information to approximate the theoretical measure of economic well-being. Differences in the empirical measures should be explainable by differences in the theoretical definitions of well-being, by differences in the information available in the specific data sets, and by differences in the empirical specification of a particular theoretical concept.

By now it should be clear that prior to evaluating a specific empirical measure of economic well-being, the theoretical definition of economic well-being must be established. In the preceding paper by Moon and Smolensky, there is some confusion about the theoretical definition of economic well-being which guides their suggestions for measuring it. They begin by suggesting that the measure should represent the family's resource constraint on the purchase of goods and services. They also specifically mention that the measure should represent "attainable consumption." However, they do not specify whether the resources of the family are to be evaluated by their market value or by the value assigned to the resources by the family. By favoring the life-cycle concept over the permanent-income concept, they do indicate that they consider the appropriate time period for their purposes to be the remaining life of the family. They do not deal with the problems of the definition of the family or of the life of the family unit. This lack of specificity in their theoretical concept of economic well-being is not unusual in this area of research. However, the lack of specificity means that there is no one standard by which to judge their suggestions about the appropriate methods for the incorporation of various resources into the measure of economic well-being.

In the following discussion of their proposed measure of economic well-being, I indicate how the methods for incorporating various assets such as home ownership and in-kind transfers depend on the specific theoretical measure of economic well-being which is being approximated. I also note some of the problems of actually adopting their suggestions in empirical work.

Home Ownership

In their discussion of the appropriate method for including home ownership in the measure of economic well-being, Moon and Smolensky argue that as long as current institutions are not developed for the smooth reduction of the consumption of housing services, the incorporation of the annuitized value of home equity in the measure of economic well-being is misleading. They prefer the adjustment of money income for the annuitized value of the imputed rent from the home.

If economic well-being is defined from an objective viewpoint, with resources valued at their market rate, I argue that the annuitized value of home equity is more appropriate. With this approach, the person with a $15,000 house is treated equivalently to the person who sold a $15,000 house and purchased an annuity, a practice not unheard of among the aged. Several researchers have suggested that this approach overstates the economic well-being of older persons who own their own homes (Morgan, 1965; Moon, 1975). These arguments implicitly adopt a definition of economic well-being which does not value resources solely in terms of their market value. In addition, the arguments assume that the market value of the home and the value of the home to the individual are not equal. One possible explanation for this apparent irrational behavior on the part of the individual is that the poor health of the older person severely limits the time available for market transactions. Ideally, this lack of healthy time would be incorporated in the measure of economic well-being by a reduction in the value of time. However, given that the reduction of time available due to poor health is not always possible in empirical specifications, the imputed rent approach can be justified as a method for indirectly adjusting the measure of economic well-being for the poor health of the older person.

Value of Time

For a number of older persons, healthy time is a primary resource. Both the considerable number of older persons who are either partially or completely retired, as well as the number of older persons whose health is rapidly depreciating, suggest the need to incorporate the value of the individual's time in both resource-based and welfare-based measures. Moon and Smolensky recognize the need to incorporate time in their measure of economic well-being, but they do not specify the appropriate method.

For the purposes of determining the contribution made by time to "attainable consumption," two alternative methods for evaluating the healthy time available to the individual can be suggested. As in the case of home ownership, the appropriate method depends, in part, on the theoretical definition of economic well-being which is being estimated. The first approach is to value the person's healthy time by the estimated average earnings of the individual assuming one worked a given proportion of one's healthy hours. This is the appropriate method if an objective measure of economic well-being with resources valued at their market price is being approximated. The second approach is to value the person's healthy time by the marginal wage for the individual's last hour worked. This is the appropriate method if the measure of economic well-being is being defined in terms of economic welfare. Unless the marginal wage and average wage are equal, the two values of time will differ. However, given the irregular income constraint facing older workers, their relationship is not known.

Although the two approaches suggested for incorporating time in measures of economic well-being are relatively simple, there are a number of issues which must be considered in developing empirical estimates of the value of time. For both methods, the potential wages of persons not working and the number of healthy hours available to the individual must be determined. Information on the potential wages of persons currently not working is generally limited to information about the market earnings of persons with similar characteristics who are working. Estimates of the number of healthy hours available to the individual are generally based on somewhat vague and subjective reports of health status by the respondent. For evaluating time using the estimated marginal wage for the individual, the discontinuity of wage offers and the irregularity of the marginal tax rates facing older workers must be considered. As suggested by the issues noted above, the incorporation of the value of time in a measure of economic well-being is generally imprecise and based on a number of assumptions that have little theoretical support. However, given the variations in both the leisure time and health status of older persons, the incorporation of the value of time in measures of economic well-being should not be neglected.

Intrafamily Transfers

Based on the recognition that parents and children frequently share resources, Moon and Smolensky suggest the need to incorporate the value of intrafamily transfers in the measure of economic well-being. If the intention is to develop a measure of "attainable resources" as stated by the authors, the incorporation of intrafamily transfers can be questioned. The person who receives in-kind transfers such as free rent generally has no claim on these resources and no control over their allocation. However, the receipt of these transfers does allow the person to attain a higher level of economic well-being both in terms of the market value of their consumption and in terms of their subjective level of well-being. Whether the incorporation of intrafamily transfers in a measure of economic well-being is desirable clearly depends on the intended use of the measure. If the measure is to be used to assess the distribution of economic welfare, then the value of intrafamily transfers should probably be included in the measure. However, if the measure is to be used to determine eligibility for a certain income maintenance program and if the policy is intended to encourage such transfers, then intrafamily transfers should probably be excluded.

Once the decision is made to include intrafamily transfers in a measure of economic well-being, there are still a number of empirical questions about the estimation of both the market value of transfers for an objective measure of well-being and the personal value assigned to transfers for a welfare-based measure. Direct information on the market value of intrafamily transfers is generally limited to reports on intrafamily monetary transfers. Indirect information can be obtained from information on the relative incomes of other family members and on the receipt of specific in-kind services, such as free rent. Estimates of the personal value assigned to these intrafamily transfers are necessarily even more imprecise. However, under most conditions the personal value will be less than the equivalent market value of the transfers. This is based on the observation that most persons receiving intrafamily transfers are only able to use the transfers for purposes approved of by the person transferring the money.

Government Transfers

Similar problems with placing a value on in-kind private transfers also exist in the evaluation of in-kind government transfers. Given that a significant proportion of the transfers made by government to older persons are in the form of in-kind services and goods, there is little doubt that the neglect of these resources understates the level of economic well-being for most all older persons. The exclusion of these benefits is also likely to overstate the differences in economic well-being between younger and older persons.

Several alternative approaches for the incorporation of in-kind benefits have been suggested (Gillespie, 1965; Moon, 1975; Schmundt et al., 1975). In-kind benefits can be evaluated by the per capita cost of the program to the government, by the equivalent market value of the resources received by the individual, and by the cash equivalent amount required to compensate the individual for the in-kind services. For estimating the value of resources allocated to specific population groups such as the elderly, the per capita cost of program is the appropriate approach. For estimating the contribution of in-kind benefits to the market resources available to the individual, the equivalent market value of resources is preferred. For the third purpose of estimating the subjective value of these in-kind benefits, estimates of the welfare compensating cash equivalent amount is the suggested approach. Under most conditions the per capita cost of program will be greater than the market equivalent value, and the market equivalent value will be greater than the utility compensating cash equivalent amount.

As suggested above, there are several alternative measures of economic well-being which are of possible interest to both the researcher and the policy-maker. In order to evaluate a specific measure of economic well-being, both the purpose of the measure and the theoretical definition of the measure must be established. Once the theoretical definition has been defined, there are still a number of empirical questions regarding the estimation of such a measure. In the above discussion, specific questions about the incorporation of home ownership, time, and private and public transfers were considered. Additional issues regarding the appropriate unit of analysis and the assumed time period have been discussed only briefly.

POLICY RECOMMENDATIONS

A primary reason for the development of measures of economic well-being is for the evaluation and formulation of social policies. Moon and Smolensky have made a number of proposals for changes in current social policies in their paper. My comments about their proposed changes are focussed on programs dealing with chronological age.

The authors specifically recommend that the "preferential treatment" of the elderly by social programs be reconsidered. I concur with this suggestion, but I would replace their term "preferential" with the word "differential." I also urge that prior to the elimination of chronological age as a criterion for eligibility in specific programs, careful scrutiny be given to the advantages of age and the possible disadvantages of the alternatives.

Despite the apparent arbitrariness of chronological age, there are a number of distinct benefits to using age that need to be recognized. First, age is a relatively inexpensive piece of information to collect in comparison to information on income, assets, or health status. Second, age is a relatively difficult piece of information to manipulate to establish one's eligibility for a program. A third advantage of chronological age is that it is somewhat impersonal. Rules that treat all persons of a given age equally do not reflect directly on the individual's mental or physical ability. A fourth possible advantage to using chronological age is that it frequently reduces the uncertainty to the individual regarding eligibility for certain benefits and exclusion from certain activities.

The relative benefits of using alternative rationing devices in place of age depend not only on the alternative rationing devices to be used, but also on the particular policy or program being considered. Currently, age is used as a screening device to determine eligibility in locally administered social service delivery programs and in nationally or state-administered cash transfer programs. Age is also used to limit access to certain jobs through mandatory retirement rules and age-based hiring standards.

In situations where service delivery programs are administered at the local level and are intended for persons with certain needs highly correlated with age, the elimination of age as a rationing device is probably not desirable. More elaborate measures of need such as assets and earnings tests are costly to administer and are thought to decrease the value of the program to the participants. However, the inclusion of all persons above a certain age in a particular program means that persons with relatively limited resources are treated the same as persons with larger resources. Possibly, the focusing of benefits on persons with limited resources would result in a greater social benefit. In these situations, the optimal situation is possibly not the elimination of age eligibility criteria but the establishment of incentives to ensure that administrators provide services to persons in the greatest need. These comments regarding the use of eligibility criteria by local service delivery programs are supported by several studies of local area agencies on aging (Tobin et al., 1976; Walther, 1976).

A second use of chronological age is in the restriction of certain jobs to persons below an established age through mandatory retirement rules and age-based hiring standards. Moon and Smolensky have suggested that the elimination of mandatory retirement rules and the enforcement and extension of laws forbidding age discrimination in hiring would increase the level of economic well-being of the older population at a relatively low cost. The recommendation about the elimination of mandatory retirement rules has been made by a number of other persons and is currently being considered by various judicial and legislative bodies. Despite this support among persons interested in improving the economic well-being of older persons, the desirability of eliminating mandatory retirement rules needs to be given careful consideration.

The use of age in determining the timing of one's retirement does seem unnecessarily arbitrary. Also, mandatory retirement rules in some but not all industries most likely lead to depressed wages in jobs without mandatory retirement rules. However, the apparently humanitarian suggestion that persons be allowed to work as long as they are "willing and able" is generally not accompanied by any suggestion as to how this system would be implemented. It is doubtful that the proposal intends to give preferential treatment to older workers or to eliminate completely the firm's control over the selection of workers. The development of new technology which can be used to determine when a person is no longer able to work for each specific job is also unlikely. Nevertheless, visions of some group of technicians deciding on when a person is "unable" to work in a specific job should be disturbing to persons concerned with the well-being and freedom of choice of older persons.

CONCLUSION

After these somewhat science fiction comments on the impact of eliminating mandatory retirement ages, I want to suggest some possible areas of research. First, the costs of using alternative eligibility criteria in place of age need to be examined. Second, the possibility of predicting the more comprehensive measures of economic well-being by a relatively simple income measure and a set of demographic characteristics should be examined. Third, the current efforts to develop and utilize measures of economic status for policy evaluation should be encouraged. For the elderly, the incorporation of the value of time and health status in the measure should be given priority. Fourth, a better understanding of the perverse impact of current policies on the economic well-being of the older population is needed.

REFERENCES

Gillespie, W.I. (1965). "Effect of Public Expenditures on the Distribution of Income," in *Essays in Fiscal Federalism*, ed. Richard A. Musgrave. Washington, D.C.: Brookings Institution.

Moon, M. (1975). *The Economic Welfare of the Aged and Income Security Programs*. Institute for Research on Poverty, Discussion Papers. Madison, Wisconsin: University of Wisconsin.

Morgan, J.N. (1965). "Measuring the Economic Status of the Aged," *International Economic Review* 6:1 (January): 1–17.

Schmundt, M., E. Smolensky, and L. Stiefel (1975). "When do Recipients Value Transfers at Their Costs to Taxpayers?" in *Integrating Income Maintenance Programs*, ed. Irene Lurie. New York: Academic Press.

Taussig, M.K. (1973). *Alternative Measures of the Distribution of Economic Welfare*. Princeton, New Jersey: Industrial Relations Section, Department of Economics, Princeton University.

Tobin, S., S.M. Davidson, and A. Sack (1976). *Models for Effective Service Delivery: Social Services for Older Americans*. Report to the Administration on Aging. Chicago, Illinois: University of Chicago.

Walther, R.J. (1976). "Eligibility Criteria and Targeting for Program Participants," in *A Longitudinal Analysis of 97 Area Agencies on Aging*, ed. Raymond M. Steinberg. Los Angeles, California: University of Southern California.

 *Chapter 3*

Integrating Social Security into an Incomes Policy

G.S. Tolley
R.V. Burkhauser

Active interest in structuring welfare measures along income-maintenance lines is at least two decades old. An appealing feature of this approach is its consideration of the total impact of government programs on the individual, leading to a unified rather than a fragmented approach to income transfer. In the present setting, where many programs exist that have grown up in isolation, a contribution of viewing programs in light of the income-maintenance approach is to suggest how to alter existing individual programs so as to enhance their contribution to overall welfare efforts. Looking further to the future, the welfare system shows signs of evolving toward a more general income-maintenance approach. A general income-maintenance approach does not rule out special programs, but it poses general income assistance as an alternative against which to test the rationale of each special program and suggests changes that would be called for in the nature of the special programs.

Social security is a key welfare program in a time when income maintenance, particularly for older persons, has been evolving rapidly. Financial stresses in the social security program, imposing the necessity to consider changes, have increased the interest in welfare measures affecting older persons. The need is therefore particularly great to consider the relation of social security to income maintenance. In dealing with the subject here, we are concerned with social security both in the context of existing programs and in the context of programs as they might be structured under a more general income-maintenance approach.

TOWARD UNIFORM TAX TREATMENT FOR PUBLIC AND PRIVATE PENSIONS

Changes in income tax provisions and in some welfare provisions are causing a more rapid evolution in the direction of an income-maintenance approach than commonly realized. Tax law changes last year included several changes in the positive tax, or regular individual income tax, at the low end of the income scale. Tax law changes have increasingly taken the poverty line as a bench mark below which income taxes will not be collected. A principal device is the minimum standard deduction, or low-income allowance, which allows a deduction from income subject to tax sufficient to relieve many persons at the low end of the income scale from federal income tax obligation. Under the tax changes last year, the minimum standard deduction was raised to $1,900 for a joint return. This means that no family of four persons with an income of $5,760 or below is subject to tax. This compares with a 1975 poverty line for such a family of about $5,500.

A concept in the design of changes in the tax law at the low end of the income scale is that it is anomalous for persons to be both receiving transfers from the government because of their poverty status and at the same time be paying income tax.

A gesture has been made toward meshing social security and income tax provisions. The "earned income credit" provides for a tax credit equal to 10 percent of earned income up to a maximum of $400 (at $4,000 of income), with a phasing down of the amount of credit as income increases such that the credit reaches zero at $8,000 of income. The credit is limited to households with at least one dependent child. This provision is designed to give back to persons at the low end of the income scale what they are contributing in social security taxes. The credit can be greater than the total income tax paid, so that persons who have worked will be compensated for social security taxes paid.

More fundamental changes are needed to bring about symmetry in tax treatment between social security and other retirement plans. Under private group pension plans, and under Individual Retirement Savings Plans (IRA) and Keogh Plans for individuals, savings in any year which are set aside for retirement are deductible from income subject to tax. The savings and the accrued earnings on them are not taxed until the time they are withdrawn in later years. This approach to savings has taken the tax system far in the direction of a general consumption tax as opposed to an income tax as such, a direction long favored to reduce the discouragement to savings that results from income tax.

Social security is treated asymmetrically under the tax laws. The employee contribution is not deductible from taxable income at the time it is made, precluding the deferral advantage on social security savings for retirement. On the other hand, social security income escapes taxation at the time it is received. This approach is another way around the tax problem with regard to savings, but it is at odds with the consumption tax approach. Given the direction the tax system is going for private savings plans, two changes called for in the tax treatment of social security are: (1) allow deduction of the employee social security contribution from income subject to tax; and (2) make social security income taxable. Allowing deductibility of all social security contributions would give further relief to persons at the low end of the income scale who under social security are taxed more heavily than persons with like income under private plans. The change would reduce pressures to opt out of the social security system. Making social security benefits taxable is a needed step in achieving coherence in income maintenance for older persons. It would eliminate the capricious tax advantage bestowed on well-to-do persons who happen to have been covered by social security. The advantage obtained from sheltering social security income from taxes is not available to lower-income persons who have little or no taxable income, nor is it available to persons who have saved for their old age but are not covered by social security. The case is strong for grouping social security income with all other income received by an individual in determining taxes and eligibility for assistance, contributing to the goal of treating persons in like circumstances alike.

THE WORK TEST

Since the receipt of full social security income before age 72 is contingent on not working, social security acts as a tax on work. This work test affects persons, many of whom are at the low end of the income scale, who would prefer to go on working but are induced to give it up to collect social security benefits. Those with large nonwork incomes are permitted to collect full social security benefits, while those who continue to work are penalized. This feature favoring higher-income people is in addition to the nontaxability of social security income that was noted in the previous section.

Besides being inequitable, the work test appears to have pronounced effects on work decisions. The fact that social security benefits are tax free while a person who elects to continue to work must pay social security taxes on wage income contributes to the high marginal tax rate on income from work for a person eligible for benefits. The marginal tax rate is the sum of the benefit loss plus all federal, state, and local taxes and the social security tax. Consider as an example a married worker who has made the median wage over his lifetime. He would have reached age 65 in 1974 with a yearly social security benefit of $4,704. If he continues to work he makes $7,723. But he would pay a 50 percent marginal tax in lost social security payments, a 17 percent marginal federal income tax, and a 5.85 percent marginal social security tax. The median worker would be subject to a 72.85 percent marginal tax rate. His average tax on earned income would be 47 percent ($3,647 total tax payment).

Bowen and Finegan (1964) and Boskin (1975), among others, have estimated that social security has been a significant influence in the fall in labor-force participation of older men. This fall has recently intensified. For example, after a relatively constant labor-force participation rate from 1948 to 1961, the labor-force participation rate for men 62–64 has fallen from about 80 percent in 1961 to 60 percent in 1975. This has happened concomitant with the relaxation of eligibility for earlier social security benefits. The proportion of men taking early social security benefits has increased from near zero to 48 percent over the period. Faster increases in social security benefits than wage rates, in the presence of the work test, have increased the advantages of retirement relative to work.

Early retirement effects have been accentuated for lower-income workers by the introduction of Supplementary Security Income (SSI) for people age 65 and over. The aim of the social security system has been to maintain a ratio of 0.8 between benefits received if initially taken at age 62 and those taken at age 65, which is a crude attempt to make the present value of benefits at ages 62 and 65 equal for a given earnings history. Table 3–1 shows benefits at age 65 for couples initially accepting benefits at 62 and 65 for various earnings levels.

For the column showing benefits without SSI, the ratio is 0.8 in every case. For the columns showing benefits including SSI, the ratio goes to 1 at the lowest earnings level and has some effect on all those whose lifetime average earnings are less than $3,150. The ratio is upset because social security is counted as income under SSI. Each additional dollar of social security is offset by the loss of a dollar of SSI. For those whose lifetime average income is less than $2,125, this means net payments at 65 are the same regardless of whether initial acceptance is at 62 or 65, that is, no decrease in annual income

Table 3–1. Income at Age 65 for Couples Accepting Social Security Payments at Ages 62 and 65 in 1974

Potential Lifetime Average Yearly Earnings as Estimated under Social Security	*Yearly Benefits with Social Security Only*			*Yearly Benefits with Social Security plus SSI*		
	Accepting Social Security at Age		*Ratio*	*Accepting Social Security at Age*		*Ratio*
	62 (a)	*65 (b)*	*(a)/(b)*	*62 (a)*	*65 (b)*	*(a)/(b)*
$923 or less	$1,352	$1,688	0.8	$2,868	$2,868	1
1,500	2,002	2,496	0.8	2,868	2,868	1
2,000	2,264	2,830	0.8	2,868	2,868	1
2,125	2,494	2,868	0.8	2,868	2,868	1
2,500	2,531	3,136	0.8	2,868	3,163	0.91
2,750	2,663	3,329	0.8	2,868	3,329	0.86
3,000	2,795	3,494	0.8	2,868	3,494	0.82
3,150	2,868	3,585	0.8	2,868	3,585	0.8
3,500	3,031	3,787	0.8	3,031	3,787	0.8

Sources: Compiled from Social Security tables.

because of early acceptance. For those with income between $2,125 and $3,150, the income floor operating on people accepting at age 62 acts to reduce the early acceptance penalty.

The method by which cost-of-living payments are added to social security benefits tilts payment toward early acceptance for all earnings level. Cost-of-living benefits are based on the worker's PIA (this is the value of the full benefit based on the worker's lifetime average wages), and not on one's actual benefit level (0.8 of one's PIA if one initially accepts at age 62). This causes the real difference between reduced early benefits and full benefits to fall with inflation. Cost-of-living changes have increased benefits by 8 percent in 1975 and 6.4 percent in 1976. If benefits rose by 5 percent in 1977, the benefit ratio will move from 0.8 to 0.836 for those who initially accepted at age 62 in 1974.

Over 15 million men between 62 and 72 years of age received social security benefits in 1974. If as few as 1 million retired early because of this combination of early social security benefits and the work test, and if the loss in production due to their exit from work averaged $5,000 per year, the loss in production was $5 billion per year. This compares with the estimate of cost to the social security system of $5 billion if the work test were removed (Ball, forthcoming).

The difference is that the $5 billion cost to the system is a transfer from one group to another. The $5 billion loss in production of the nation is a cost which nobody gains. It is an absolute loss, not just a transfer. As the health of those surviving to older ages improves, making the work-retirement choice a viable option for more persons, and as the proportion of the population in older age groups increases, the magnitude of production lost as a result of the work test will increase. The work test narrows choices and exacerbates the growing problem of what life-styles will be chosen by older persons. For many, and perhaps the majority of older persons, the work option will contribute more to the sense of worth and well-being in later years than will retirement.

An income-maintenance approach transfers income according to a means test which considers a person's total resources. The social security work-test provision is a different kind of means test which considers only earnings from work, with resulting anomalous effects. It should be emphasized that income maintenance itself may have pronounced work effects. The experimental evidence indicating the opposite has tended to deal with persons who are inelastic in supply to the labor force, such as male household heads aged 25 to 55. It may have a more powerful effect among groups marginal to the labor force, such as older persons deciding whether to retire earlier or later. One of the more prominent criticisms of the recent government experiments is their short-run nature. The wealth effect of a true lifetime guaranteed income program will be greater than that generated by a short-run experimental program, so the wealth effect is understated. Beyond the scope of this paper is the need to examine further the labor-force participation effects of income maintenance. But for low-income earners, income maintenance at least leaves open the option to work, and unlike social security it has little or no effect on the work effort of middle- and upper-income persons.

DISENTANGLING THE ANNUITY AND DISTRIBUTIVE EFFECTS OF SOCIAL SECURITY

The biggest recent step toward an income-maintenance approach has been aimed at older people and therefore has particularly great implications for social security. SSI, or Supplementary Security Income for the Aged, Blind, and Disabled—a direct income maintenance program for those over 65—has been in existence for two years. As with social security, benefits are tied to the Consumers Price Index. Under the most recent SSI benefit increase, the income floor for an aged couple is $3,022 per year. Under the SSI income-support scale, benefits are reduced by 50 percent on every dollar of earned income above the floor, up to a break-even point of about $6,500. It has a 100 percent reduction on all unearned income (private pensions, social security, and so on) after the first $240 of unearned income per year. Unlike social security, SSI is funded by general revenues. States have the option of increasing benefits, which are not considered income under SSI. The $3,022 federal minimum income floor is significantly increased by these additional supplements in many states. For the first time a significant portion of the population is covered by a full-fledged negative income tax program.

SSI has so far been a relatively inexpensive program, partly because not all those eligible have applied for benefits, and more importantly because other programs including social security already provide much income support for older persons. SSI is a general income-maintenance program that fills in gaps left by a set of large programs already in existence.

The question becomes, What would be the implications of making SSI the major program instead of the residual, that is, making SSI the cornerstone of income support for older persons and bringing in other programs to meet special needs not met by SSI? Now that SSI is in existence, this change is a logical next step in achieving a unified approach to income maintenance for older persons.

To answer the question requires explicit recognition that social security as it now exists is a mixture of an annuity and a welfare program. The guaranteed payment which social security provides after age 62 is similar to an annuity. If its sole purpose were to provide an annuity, the program would function in the same way as do private annuity plans. Out of earnings during earlier years of life, an individual would purchase a guaranteed income stream that would start at some future date. Under such a program, the present value of the payments is equal to the expected present value of the income stream. There is a direct relationship between payments made and benefits received, with neither a gain nor a loss in lifetime wealth position from being in the program.

Because it was clear that many families would be hard pressed to purchase an actuarial annuity of this kind, the social security program was designed to include redistributive features that would enable poorer workers to obtain higher relative returns on their payments. The design of the social security system included other redistributive departures from annuity principles that are less clearly justified on egalitarian grounds. In the end, the social security system emerges as a hybrid between an annuity mechanism and a redistributive mechanism, with the redistributive mechanism having both egalitarian and anti-egalitarian features.

To mention only some of the redistributive features, under social security a single person and a married person whose partner does not work in the market can have the same work histories but will receive different benefits. The yearly benefits for the married person is 50 percent higher than for the single person. As another example, in estimating social security benefits, the wage history of the higher earner of a married couple is used. The benefits for the couple are increased 50 percent, regardless of the other partner's earnings. The 50 percent bonus for marriage and the ignoring of the wife's earnings in determining benefits limits women's independence and discriminates against married women entering the labor force.

The replacement ratio concept—that a worker's benefit should be some specified fraction of the income that was being earned just before retirement—is another departure from the annuity principle. The annuity principle fits in with the idea that savings for retirement are motivated by desires to even out consumption over the lifetime, giving back to each worker all savings plus interest accrued. In principle the replacement-ratio concept takes a shorter view and arbitrarily favors those whose incomes peak just before retirement.

The basic requirement for fully integrating social security into a general income-maintenance program is to ensure that a consistent set of redistribution procedures is followed. Two approaches may be mentioned. The approaches would be identical in their effects, differing only in paperwork. The first approach would require changing the redistributive features of social security to conform with the redistributive features of the general income-maintenance program. For instance, in determining social security benefits, the total resources rather than work income alone would be considered, using the same negative tax rate schedule as the general income-maintenance program. The second approach would be to drop entirely the redistributive features of social security, converting social security to a program based on actuarial annuity principles and letting the redistributive function be carried out through the general income-maintenance program.

THE NEED FOR SOCIAL SECURITY UNDER GENERAL INCOME MAINTENANCE

If redistributive functions were taken over by general income maintenance, and if social security were converted into an actuarial program offering annuities on the same basis as private programs, would there be any reason still to have social security? A generally overlooked consideration is that, if there is a substantial income-maintenance program that covers older persons, one of the major motives for saving will be weakened.

Consider those persons whose savings in the absence of income maintenance would give them an income in old age less than the income-maintenance floor. They will have their motives to save for old age abolished. They can have the same income as they had planned in old age without undertaking any savings for it at all. Consider now those persons whose savings would put them above the floor, but not above maximum benefits. They will be subject to a bribe not to save. Because of the existence of income maintenance that will supplement their privately financed consumption according to a negative tax rate schedule, the return to each dollar of their own saving effort will be reduced. They can be expected to save less than they otherwise would, and perhaps substantially less.

A case can be made for a mandatory universal minimum annuity program to accompany general income maintenance, in order to offset the incentives to reduce savings under an income-maintenance program. The major incentive to reduce savings has been instituted with SSI, since it applies universally to older persons. If SSI were extended to become applicable to persons of all ages, there might be some further effects on savings, but it is not clear that they would be important in comparison to the effects already engendered by the income guarantee for old age.

A logical role for social security in the presence of SSI or other general income maintenance is to provide annuities required as universal minimums. The minimums would vary according to income up to a largest minimum requirement. The largest minimum requirement would be chosen to correspond to that income level above which deleterious effects of income maintenance on savings are deemed unlikely. The annuities would be offered on actuarial principles (present value of payments into the annuity equal to present value of benefits). Anyone would have the option of purchasing a private annuity of at least equal amount. The private option would be typical for higher-income persons who of their own volition would be covered by their own saving and pension plans above their required minimum. The social security program would be smaller than at present for two reasons. First, it would most likely be used less by higher-income people than it is now. Second, it would be subject to private competition which might satisfy some or even all of the required demand for annuities.

Consideration might be given to guaranteeing returns in real terms, providing insurance against inflation. This could be done through lending the savings of annuities to investors by offering to buy purchasing power bonds, so that the borrower would take the risks associated with unanticipated inflation instead of the lender as is typical under present financial arrangements.

It should be emphasized that this discussion concerns the effects on savings of income maintenance and not the effect of the present social security system on savings. Regarding the effects of the present social security system, if social security taxes and benefits were operated as part of the general government budget, payees would increase their savings if the required contributions put them above what they would otherwise be saving. Recipients of benefits in old age would be consuming more in old age than in the absence of the program. Assuming government expenditures were unaffected, the net effect on savings of the nation would depend on the relative magnitude of the changes in spending behavior of the payees and beneficiaries. The effect would change over time as the age composition of the population changed.

With an "unfunded" system nominally separate from the general government budget, but where any excess of system receipts over payments is held in the form of government securities, the holdings of securities outside of government are just as they would be if the system were operated as part of the general government budget. There is no reason to expect the effects on savings of the nation to be any different in the two cases.

If now the system were funded through putting the proceeds of the social security payments into private securities, the effect as compared to either of the previous two cases would be to exchange private securities for government securities; that is, government debt held in the private sector would have to increase in order to enable the purchase of the private securities. Again, there is no reason to expect this portfolio adjustment involving the exchange of two types of securities at market value to affect savings behavior. Thus, regardless of the method of financing, it appears the effects of social security on saving are the same.

These conclusions differ from Feldstein (1974; 1975), who argues that funding will increase savings, and they differ at least in degree from the Barro (1974) and Miller and Upton (1974) arguments that bequest motives make for zero effect of social security on savings. The argument here is that social security requirements can make savings greater than they otherwise would be and indeed are needed for just this purpose in the presence of income-maintenance programs. The argument rests on the assumption that lower-income people have imperfect options for reducing their savings in other forms if required to purchase an annuity, because they would otherwise have less financial savings than required by the annuity and because possibilities for disinvesting in children who might later support them are limited.

STRATEGIES FOR CHANGE

This paper has not examined the magnitude of income redistribution but rather has considered principles that are applicable to any amount of redistribution. The main result of the changes would be to make more rational and effective the way that government impinges on individuals. The discussion has been an exercise in finding guiding principles, deliberately ignoring the likelihood of enactment of the various changes.

The changes outlined are an agenda for improvement that could be offered together or individually on occasions when there are small or large reconsiderations of the social security system. Making social security contributions deductible from income, taxing social security benefits, and eliminating the work test are changes of not too great magnitude that it would be appropriate to make at any time. It could also be appropriate to revise on a piecemeal basis the various redistributive provisions of the social security system to bring them more in conformance with general income-maintenance programs.

Taking the full step toward a universal minimum annuity requirement based solely on actuarial principles is a drastic change unlikely to be considered short of an upheaval of the system. It would be appropriate to consider this step as one of the options for reform if aid from general funds were to become necessary to save the system.

REFERENCES

Ball, Robert (forthcoming). "Income Security After Retirement," in *Social Policy, Social Ethics, and the Aging*, ed. Bernice Neugarten.

Barro, Robert (1974). "Are Government Bonds Net Wealth?" *Journal of Political Economy* (November/December).

Boskin, Michael (1975). "Social Security and Retirement Decisions." Working Paper, National Bureau of Economic Research, *Workshop on Pension Research.*

Bowen, William, and Thomas Finegan (1969) *The Economics of Labor Force Participation*. Princeton, New Jersey.

Feldstein, Martin (1975). "Social Security and Payroll Savings: International Evidence in an Extended Life-Cycle Model." Working Paper, National Bureau of Economic Research, *Workshop on Pension Research.*

____ (1974). "Social Security Induced Retirement and Aggregate Capital Accumulation," *Journal of Political Economy* 82: 5 (September/October).

Miller, Merton H., and Charles Upton (1974). *Macroeconomics: A Neoclassical Introduction.* Homewood, Illinois: Irvin.

Commentary

Comment on Tolley and Burkhauser

Lawrence H. Thompson

Although the social security benefit structure has always combined elements of redistribution (a "welfare component") with elements of retirement insurance (an "annuity component"), the relative importance of these two components has changed through the years. Over the four decades since the inception of the program, almost every legislated change in its benefit structure has served to enhance the welfare component at the expense of the annuity component. Many now argue that the time has come to halt and reverse this trend. In their paper "Integrating Social Security into an Incomes Policy," Tolley and Burkhauser ask whether the trend away from an annuity-based social security benefit should be reversed and, based on an economic argument, they conclude that it should. Later in this volume John Palmer will ask whether the trend is likely to be reversed and, based on a political argument, he will conclude that it will.

In large part the recent interest in restructuring the social security program can be traced to the replacement in 1972 of the Aid to the Aged, Blind, and Disabled grant-in-aid programs with the Supplemental Security Income program. The SSI program is a federally administered, means tested, cash assistance program which is not only targeted at virtually the same population as is served by social security, but is administered by the same agency from the same network of local offices.

With the creation of SSI, we now have a vehicle, if in some regards an imperfect one, for making our welfare transfers more explicit and

The views expressed in this paper are those of the author and do not necessarily reflect the views of the Department of Health, Education and Welfare.

more target efficient and for financing them from the general revenues rather than from the payroll tax. Naturally this raises questions about the wisdom of continuing certain features of the social security system. It also raises questions about the operation of our entire income-maintenance system for the elderly—about the desirability of the net effect of the interaction of the two programs.

In these comments I shall begin by discussing the likely effect of the creation of SSI and of other recent developments on the nature of the social security program. I will then examine several ways in which SSI and social security interact, pointing out some results I consider to be undesirable. Unfortunately, I have not yet worked out a satisfactory answer to these problems, so I can not offer any solutions. I will close with a couple of observations about specific proposals for change that affect the social security program.

THE LIKELY FUTURE ROLE OF SOCIAL SECURITY

In their discussion of the role that social security might play in an ideal world, Tolley and Burkhauser ask whether, in fact, the program needs to exist at all.

> If the redistributive functions were taken over by general income maintenance, and if social security were converted into an actuarial program offering annuities on the same basis as private programs, would there be any reason still to have social security?

Tolley and Burkhauser go on to supply an affirmative answer to that question, noting the need to offset the retirement saving disincentive that is created among potential SSI recipients. But they also note that the social security system which is required for this purpose would be a rather trivial operation in comparison to the size and scope of today's system. The system they envision is one in which any individual who can show sufficient private retirement savings in a given year may opt out of the social security system. Social security is left as the residual annuity program for those who do not make other provisions.

As long as we are discussing social security in a world that is unfettered by previous history, I can agree with this conclusion. In fact, I am not convinced that in such a world we would even need the abbreviated social security system that Tolley and Burkhauser suggest. It may be sufficient to mandate the purchase of private annuities, require sellers of these annuities to purchase a government-sponsored insurance against default, and, perhaps, offer a subsidy or tax rebate to the poor to help them finance their purchase.

At the same time, while it is fine to discuss how income maintenance for the aged might work in an idealized world, focusing our attention on that topic can cause us to overlook some important questions about how the income-maintenance system should work in the world in which we should really expect to find ourselves living. It is my contention—and I have no reason to believe that Tolley and Burkhauser disagree—that in the practical world, the social security program is not going to go away, and we will therefore have to face the task of rationalizing its interaction with other elements of the income maintenance system.

I am willing to go on the record with three assertions about what the social security system is going to look like in the next 25 to 50 years. First, no matter what the future may hold in the way of alterations to the social security benefit structure, the aggregate size of the program, aggregate benefit outlays as a percent of GNP, is not going to shrink very much. Second, the system is not going to be made voluntary and it is not going to be fully funded. Third, although the relative size of the welfare component of social security may be reduced, it will not be eliminated.

When we set up the social security system, we made the decision to finance social security benefits on a less than full reserve basis. This decision has allowed us to pay benefits to a generation of retirees which were far in excess of the value of the taxes that these retirees had paid. At the same time, as some of the critics of the system are fond of pointing out, it also allowed us to run up an unfunded liability to the present generation of workers that amounts to some $2-3 trillion. That unfunded liability represents the price tag to the current working generation which is associated with either fully funding or eliminating the present social security system. It is a cost which current workers can largely avoid if the policy of current cost financing can be continued. I suggest that very few people in our society are so upset with the way the social security system now operates that they are willing to pay the price required to terminate it.

It is generally agreed that a current cost financed social security system can afford to pay a rate of return which is equal to the rate of growth of average wages plus the rate of growth of population. Unfortunately, we as a society will soon face one of the consequences of a declining rate of growth of population. Barring some improbable reversal in birth rates, we shall find the ratio of retirees-to-workers rising rather dramatically in the first third of the twenty-first century. The unfavorable impact on social security costs of this shift in the population structure will offset the favorable impact of real wage growth for a period of some 20 years, in effect eliminating any real return on social security taxes. Thus, several cohorts of workers cannot expect to obtain as great a rate of return from the present social security system as they would from a fully funded alternative. Were these workers given the choice of opting out of the social security system, it would be to their individual advantage to do so. However, these same workers would probably find that the result of their collectively opting out of the system would be to lower the rate of return they earn on their total retirement taxes and savings. This is because a collective opting out of the system would force the paying off of the unfunded liability. Thus, given the population projections, it appears that the social security program cannot be allowed to become a voluntary program.

With regard to the objections to the current role of the welfare component in social security, I think it is interesting to note that almost all of the current criticism of the program's benefit structure is focused on perceived horizontal inequities rather than on perceived vertical inequities. These horizontal inequities include the differences between the treatment of men and the treatment of women, the differences between the treatment of households which have had the same aggregate wage income but derived it from two earners instead of one, and the perception that some persons with adequate retirement incomes derived from noncovered employment are benefiting unfairly as a result of qualifying for a social security benefit containing a hefty dose of the welfare component. In each of these instances, I would characterize the criticism as being that of a situation in which households that have made equal payments for social security (or a competing public retirement program) are not obtaining equal retirement benefits.

One does hear objections to the present benefit structure that can be characterized as criticisms of its vertical equity, but there is no clear pattern to these criticisms. On the one hand, some would urge that we do away with the minimum benefit entirely, and others would favor reducing or eliminating the progressivity of the first bracket of the benefit formula. On the other hand, there appears to be equally strong support for generating additional social security revenues through the institution of an ad hoc wage base increase, a move which reduces the long-run deficit only because it increases the amount of redistribution in the benefit structure.

As I see it, social security is basically a program through which the middle class insures itself against the loss of wage income resulting from the occurrence of several quite common, and in some cases inevitable, events. Certainly the majority of the participants want the program structure to return them the best rate of return they can obtain, and most want it structured so that they and persons they perceive to be their equals are treated as equals. But I see no reason to believe that the middle class will not structure the program so that those who are perceived to be better off than they are will be required to subsidize those who are perceived to be worse off than they are. Thus, if I had to guess where the social security program is likely to go, I would guess that it will be in the direction of paying current cost financed "relative annuities." Families making equal tax payments will receive roughly equal rates of return on these benefits, but the rate of return will vary with the size of the contributions made. Within this framework, I would not be surprised to see some diminishing of the vertical redistribution in the program, but I would be surprised to see it completely eliminated.

INTEGRATING SOCIAL SECURITY AND SSI

If we assume that the social security program will continue to exist in something like its present form, the significance of the SSI program is that we are now simultaneously operating two transfer programs aimed at serving the same population. One is not means tested, is designed to pay a wage-related benefit, and is financed from payroll tax revenues. The other is means tested, is designed to guarantee a minimum level of consumption, and is financed from the general revenues.

Integrating these two programs requires that we examine the net effect of the simultaneous operation of both programs on the aged. The challenge is to organize the two programs so that, to the extent possible, they achieve together all of the goals which each was intended to achieve individually. These goals include:

1. Assuring that each aged individual can afford a minimum level of consumption.
2. Making any welfare-type transfers as target efficient as possible and, to the extent possible, financing them in a progressive manner.
3. Preserving an incentive for retirement savings and for work effort.
4. Providing for some scaling of the size of retirement benefits to previous earnings levels.

The current social security and SSI programs interact in such a way that the first of these four goals is the only one which is adequately served by the present income security system.

At present, when an individual qualifies for payments from both the social security and SSI programs, the social security payment is treated as the primary payment and the SSI payment is treated as the residual payment; that is, the size of one's social security payment does not depend on the size of one's SSI payment. It is the SSI payment that is adjusted to reflect the social security income.

Moreover, under the current SSI computation rules, social security benefits, as well as all other sources of unearned income, are taxed at a marginal rate of 100 percent. The first $20 per month of this income is disregarded and the SSI benefit is then reduced by all of the additional amount of unearned income. The effect of this is to make the total income of persons who are receiving benefits under both programs completely independent of the size of their social security benefits.

The second of the goals noted above was to make welfare-type transfers as target efficient as possible and to finance them in a progressive manner. Given the way the SSI and social security programs are structured, they certainly do not do a very adequate job of furthering this goal. Since the SSI program pays the residual benefit, the only effect of creating the SSI program has been to fill whatever needs for a means-tested benefit had been left unmet by the previous Aid to the Aged. Target efficiency has been increased to the extent that needy persons were not previously served adequately. But there has been no decrease in the target inefficiency produced by making welfare-type transfer payments to persons who do not really need them. There has been no change in the size or target efficiency of any welfare component of social security, and there has been no shifting of the costs of this component onto the general revenues. Tolley and Burkhauser clearly favor such a shifting, and, notwithstanding my views on the likelihood of it occurring to the extent we would like, I also favor such a shifting.

The third of the goals was the preserving of work and savings incentives. The earnings-test provision in the social security program and the earned income disregard provisions in the SSI program are each designed to preserve some incentive to work. However, as Tolley and Burkhauser have shown, the effect of the interaction of the two programs is an unplanned elimination of most of the presumed neutrality of the actuarial reduction in social security. And, to the extent that the SSI population can be expected to save, the current provisions of that program clearly remove all of the incentive to do so.

The fourth goal was to provide some degree of scaling of retirement income levels to previous wage levels. This goal can be seen explicitly in the benefit computation procedures of the present social security program. However, for those households eligible for SSI, the effect of any scaling of social security benefits is completely offset by the effect of the SSI benefit. With regard to a significant fraction of the population, the fourth goal is completely defeated by the SSI program.

The data in Table 1 are rough estimates of the magnitude of several of the effects discussed here. These data are based on a preliminary version of the 1973 Current Population Survey—Summary Earnings Record Exact Match File which is being constructed jointly by the Census Bureau and the Social Security Administration. They are estimates of the way the SSI and social security program would have interacted during calendar 1973.

In the table, all of the matched Current Population Survey households which contained at least one person who was over 65 and receiving social security benefits were categorized by the level of the social security average monthly wage (AMW). Married couples consisting of two workers, each of whom is actually drawing a retired worker's benefit, were categorized by the sum of their AMWs. The first bracket contains all of the households that have AMWs below $76. These are the household's which are drawing the minimum benefit.

The second and third columns of the table show the estimated total number of households in each bracket and the percentage of the total number in the sample who fall in or below the bracket. The next columns show the 1973 social security benefit paid to the mean household in each bracket, the SSI benefit (exclusive of any state supplement) to which the mean household is entitled, and the total income of the household. The final column shows the fraction of the households in each bracket which are eligible to draw an SSI benefit.

The data in Table 1 suggest that the SSI program does in fact serve to offset much of the scaling of social security benefits which occurs at the lower AMW levels. For instance, the mean social security benefit rises by $480 between the first and sixth ($136–$150) brackets, but mean total transfer income rises by only $180. The effect of the SSI program is to offset almost two-thirds of the increase in social security benefits. In 1973, about one-third of the households containing a social security recipient 65 or over fell within the range in which this occurred.

These results also illustrate the potential that exists for transferring expenditures from the social security trust funds to the general revenues. About 20 percent of the social security recipients in the entire

Table 1. Effect of The Interaction of SSI and Social Security on the Distribution of Social Security Benefit Payments
(simulated effect of an SSI program in calendar 1973)[a]

Average Monthly Wage	No. of Households (thousands)	Cumulative Percent Distribution	Mean Annual Income of Households in Bracket				Percent of Households Qualifying For SSI
			Social Security	SSI	Total Transfer	Total[b] Income	
Under $76	2,089	14%	$1,238	$400	$1,639	$2,818	54%
$ 77– 90	801	20	1,360	332	1,693	2,865	55
91–105	554	24	1,455	266	1,721	2,783	53
106–120	470	27	1,577	204	1,761	3,090	50
121–135	404	30	1,682	126	1,808	3,518	39
136–150	402	32	1,718	100	1,818	3,477	33
151–165	389	35	1,796	78	1,874	3,223	35
166–180	364	38	1,843	58	1,901	3,635	30
181–195	368	40	1,915	40	1,955	3,667	22
196–210	329	42	1,948	35	1,983	3,179	16
211–225	370	45	2,098	20	2,118	3,754	5
226–240	323	47	2,180	10	2,190	4,114	3
240–255	354	50	2,204	11	2,215	3,992	3
over 255	7,330	100	3,052	6	3,058	6,805	1
Entire Sample	14,547		$2,332	$108	$2,440	$5,017	20%

[a] Although the SSI program was enacted in 1972, the first benefit was not paid until January 1974. These estimates are based on the assumption that the SSI program existed in 1973 in the same form as it was enacted in 1972. In this form, the guarantee for a single individual is $120 per month. In actuality, the single individual guarantee was raised to $140 just before the first payments were made.

[b] I followed the SSI accounting conventions in computing total household income. Thus, the figure is the income of only those persons over age 65 or of those persons married to people over age 65.

Source: Computations based on preliminary version of CPS–SER exact match file.

sample would have qualified for SSI benefits and would have found, in effect, that the size of their social security benefit did not affect their total transfer entitlement. In the aggregate, these social security beneficiaries received $3.5 billion in social security benefits and $1.6 billion in SSI payments. The $3.5 billion paid them from the social security trust fund amounted to about 8 percent of all 1973 social security retirement and survivor payments.

Finally, the column showing the percentage of persons in each bracket who would have qualified for an SSI payment can be taken as a crude indicator of the target efficiency of certain welfare features in social security. Of particular interest is the fact that only about 50 percent of the households with AMWs in the lower quartile of the AMW distribution—those with AMWs below $120—qualified for SSI. This would suggest that the tilt in the PIA computation formula which favors this group is not terribly target efficient.

OTHER PROPOSALS FOR REFORM

In their paper, Tolley and Burkhauser make a number of suggestions for reforming the social security system. I shall conclude by commenting on two of these: (1) the rebate of payroll tax payments for low income workers, where I generally agree with their position; and (2) the earnings test, where I generally disagree with their position.

Earned Income Credit

I thought their characterization of the earned income credit as a "gesture" was particularly apt. At the present time, this credit is available only to those households which include dependent children. If you do not have a dependent child living with you, you don't get the tax credit. Moreover, the credit applies to any earned income. Its availability is not dependent on that earned income having come from employment covered by the social security system. Finally, the provision is due to expire this year. Clearly, as a scheme for rebating social security payroll taxes, the earned income credit has some serious flaws.

Eventually we shall have to find some method for offsetting the burden of the payroll tax on low-income households. The need for such a tax relief scheme will increase if it turns out that the vertical redistribution within the social security benefit formula is reduced.

The only practical way of achieving payroll tax relief appears to be through the use of a provision in the personal income tax. For one thing, payroll taxes cannot be made progressive at the point of their collection because no single employer can know what an individual's total annual wages will be. For another, the use of the income tax is the only way to target the rebate to low-income households and not give it also to secondary workers whose low annual earnings need not imply a low total household income.

Earnings Test

The emerging conventional wisdom among economists seems to be that the earnings test ought to be eliminated. I do not agree with this assessment, although I am not prepared to say that there is not an alternative that is to be preferred to the present arrangement.

I am sure that few people would argue with the contention that one effect of the social security system has been to reduce labor-force participation among the elderly. In and of itself, however, this should not be considered undesirable. The whole purpose of the social security system is to give to the aged the resources necessary to allow them to stop working. The system is based on the presumption that the utility of the production loss involved in retirement is less than the welfare loss involved in having to work until one drops dead.

The social security system affects the labor-force behavior of the elderly both through its income effect and its substitution effect. Presumably, the income effect is the effect that was intended when the system was instituted and is no more objectionable than is the income effect of having an Individual Retirement Account. What is objectionable is the substitution effect produced by the earnings test.

If the only thing at issue in considering the earnings test were its effect on economic efficiency, I too would favor its elimination. But the elimination of the earnings test also has implications for the equity of the system.

The result of simply eliminating the earnings test would be to eliminate all pretenses about a person having to retire in order to receive retirement benefit. The social security retirement program would then become a wage-related, age-conditioned demogrant, paying some workers a rather substantial income supplement based simply on the fact that they have managed to live to age 65 (or 62). Whenever I try to envision the social security program without any test of retirement, I get hung up on the picture of a worker paying taxes to finance a supplement to the income of his higher-paid supervisor (plus one for the supervisor's spouse and one to each of their dependents). I find this an unacceptable result.

If you are concerned about both equity and efficiency, there is no good solution to the dilemma presented by this trade-off. The equity consideration dictates that an individual do something which can be characterized as retirement before benefits are paid, and whatever that test is, it must inevitably create a substitution effect against work. The present arrangement may sacrifice too much in efficiency for what it achieves in equity, but I believe that to do away with the earnings test entirely would be to sacrifice too much in equity for what is achieved in efficiency. The only change I can think of that would further both goals but still not answer all of the objections to the present earnings test would be to institute an actuarial increase in the benefit due persons who work after age 65.

Chapter 4

Pensions in a General Scheme of Income Transfers

Nelson McClung

An analysis of program combined impacts on disposable incomes of families must convince anyone that the American scheme of income transfers is rich in unintended effects. These unintended effects are the consequence, first, of tinkering with programs on the basis of partial information. But that tinkering has created a structure of program interrelationships so complex that policy-makers now simply cannot know what they are doing in changing this or that program. And the task of analyzing proposed tax and grant policy changes has become exceedingly complex. The Treasury now maintains a transfer income model which is a computer program with over 50,000 Fortran source statements and, at the Treasury and elsewhere, about twenty people work full time adding every day to the scope and detail of the model.

The preeminent challenge of the American scheme for taking income from some and giving it to others is rationalizing the system. The system comprises two sorts of programs. There are wage-replacement programs, which require or provide opportunities for a family to average income over its lifetime. Then there are income-support programs, which each time period average income over all or some families. The primary concern in this review of policy issues is with the wage-replacement programs. I identify eight issues. In one or another context, all are issues of program coordination.

1. Is there some way to define the public interest in wage replacement such that, if OASI and employee pension plans together provide that rate of replacement for a worker, we can say that the public

interest is satisfied? Obviously this rule includes that case in which combined OASI grants and employee pensions exceed the standard, but I reserve that for Topic 8. My concern here is with shortfalls. Perhaps a third of workers have effective employee plan coverage, in the sense that, when they retire, they will receive an employee plan supplement to OASI from one or more plans. The weighting of the OASI Primary Insurance Amount (PIA) computation in favor of those with low average monthly earnings (AME) may be interpreted as an attempt to adjust upward the rate of wage replacement for those uncovered by employee plans relative to the combined fate for those who are. It is a crude adjustment, for many lower-paid workers have employee plan coverage and many higher-paid workers do not have coverage—effective coverage, that is—and there are those without even nominal coverage.

Instead of weighting the PIA computation to give higher grant/AME ratios to those with lower AME, why should not the Social Security Administration be authorized and funded to promote the development of multi-employer plans, especially those like the plans of the Teamsters and Machinists, which are not industry specific. Funding requirements and, hence, current contributions costs could be kept down through a pension indemnity fund managed by the Social Security Administration, which would assume ultimate liability for the pension obligations of the plans. Alternatively, the Social Security Administration could develop and offer to employers and employees its own supplemental plans.

The objective would be to assure that OASI and employee plans together provide, for nearly all workers with substantial labor-force participation, a rate of wage replacement that is close to the standard set by the public-interest criterion. Supplementation, of course, should be voluntary. We are concerned here with two limits: the upper limit of combined OASI and employee plan replacement, beyond which we say that the public has no significant interest in actual rates of replacement, and the lower limit set by OASI replacement, which we consider of such paramount importance that we compel participation in the plan which provides that rate.

2. Are there any objective criteria for determining when the range of ratios of grants to contributions is excessive? Because both OASI and employee retirement plans typically provide only life annuities and not annuities certain, there is some question about the legitimacy of computations of rates of return on contributions. Nevertheless, both types of plans create values similar to property values. The property is nontransferable and not convertible to cash except subject to rather severe restrictions. However, that many people at least do assign some value to these rights is evidenced by their willingness to bargain current money wages and pay FICA taxes for them. Whatever difficulty lawyers may have in defining worker equities in employee plan or OASI pension promises, to economists the value of these property rights is simply the future current value of the benefits promised discounted for timing and uncertainty of receipt. But it does seem strange that some people can buy a better right for a given contribution than can others.

Current differentials in the prices at which these peculiar property rights can be bought are not well understood. We need a study that includes in the analysis federal and state income tax treatments of contributions and grants. Although it is a fact that the OASI PIA computation is weighted in favor of persons with low AME, a rate-of-return calculation on an after-tax basis might well reveal that, just with respect to OASI, system redistribution is from poor to rich. Considering employee pensions along with OASI, the likelihood of upstream redistribution is greater. If we assume that both FICA taxes and employee plan contributions are borne by covered workers, then OASI is financed half from before- and half from after-tax income; employee plans usually are financed entirely from before-tax income. Taxing the portion of the grant that is not a return of contributions does not reduce the rate of return very much as compared to other placements of funds, because the deferral of tax is for so long that the interest earnings on the deferred taxes essentially pay the taxes. In this respect, employee plans are favored over OASI. On the other hand, OASI grants are entirely exempt from tax. For persons with large incomes in retirement, this complete exemption can make OASI an attractive placement. Nevertheless, it is worth keeping in mind that the federal income tax subsidy to employee plans through exemption of employer contributions and interest earnings net of taxes on grants is at least equal to the subsidy to OASI through exemption of grants. This is true for current years. On projections which we now think are reasonable, it will not be true in years well off into the future.

3. To what extent does the existence of the program of Supplemental Security Income compromise the rationale for OASDI system redistribution? The rationale is what is referred to as social adequacy. Presumably this means that as a society we think that as a consequence of retirement, disability, or survivorship, people should not live at incomes which are too low. Thus, a program whose basic rationale is preventing people from living at incomes which are too low relative to their past incomes is transformed into a program with the subordinate objective of preventing some people from living at incomes whichare too low relative to the incomes of others. That compassionate communism which we cannot achieve for the active we seek for the inactive. But SSI provides a floor of income support for the aged and disabled. Why should we not return OASDI to the principle of the original act (never implemented) of individual equity?

One reason is budgetary appearances. Presently, in the computation of SSI grants (with a minor exception), OASDI grants reduce SSI grants dollar for dollar. This, in effect, shifts the cost of income floor support from general revenues to the OASDI trust funds. Were SSI grants to reduce OASDI grants dollar for dollar, a substantial part of the cost of floor support would be shifted from the trust funds to general revenues. In either case, persons eligible for SSI do or would pay FICA taxes for nothing. Reducing an OASDI grant by 50 cents for each dollar of SSI grant would leave an SSI recipient with a rate of return on FICA contributions which compares favorably with rates of return received by OASDI beneficiaries whose retirement, disability, and survivorship income is too high for them to be eligible for SSI. But this would shift grant costs to general taxpayers, and one of the fundamental principles of OASDI is that it is the middle- and lower-income classes who are relieved by these programs of supporting their relatives when they are unable to support themselves, and so it is the middle and lower classes who should pay. Perhaps this is the real reason for loading income floor costs onto the trust funds. The result, of course, is redistribution primarily from the middle- to the lower-income classes, the upper-income classes contributing much less than in proportion to what is usually considered their ability to pay.

4. Should the Social Security Administration begin planning for OASDI to become a residual program, primary responsibility for wage replacement in the events of retirement, disability, and survivorship being assumed by employee plans? However an analysis of pension rates of return might come out, it does seem that higher-paid state government workers think that they can get a better return on own and employer contributions through their employee pension plans than on contributions paid into OASDI. The more private plans are improved through collective bargaining and legislation, the more certain it is that the urge to opt out will increasingly infect private employees. Private employees cannot do so now, but one easily can imagine that Congress would permit private employees to leave the

OASDI system if their will to do so were strong enough and they could show effective and adequate employee plan coverage. High current costs projected for OASDI will strengthen the motive to opt out. For many years current costs for OASDI will rise, while current costs for employee plans will fall, because, with advance in contrast to current funding, interest earnings come increasingly to finance the grants promised.

It does seem that for many years into the future OASDI will operate in a world of well-funded employee plans. Being well funded, these plans will be able to liberalize benefits from additions to the ratio of contributions to payroll that will still leave them with current contributions rates that are low compared to the FICA tax rates required to finance OASDI. Even if comparisons of after-tax rates of return should turn out favorable to OASDI and OASDI benefits remain tax exempt, employers and employees may still desire the good things that can be bought through the employee plan with released FICA taxes. For workers having effective employee plan coverage, employee plans will become a superior means for the provision of wage replacement when they retire, become disabled, or die. Perhaps OASDI, or at least OASI, should start going out of business. For a long transition it could serve, of course, in the role that it has had since its origin of providing replacement income for persons without adequate employee plan coverage. It is worth remarking that just such thoughts as these run through the heads of federal civil employees whenever the question of integrating the U.S. Civil Service Retirement System and OASDI come up. OASDI system redistribution in fact does undermine support for it among better-paid workers; yet, holding the loyalty of these people is essential to the continuance of OASDI near universal coverage and the possibility of financing system redistribution. It may well be the case that OASDI can retain the capacity to redistribute only if it does not use it.

5. Is there any way to determine what is the optimum aggregate burden of wage replacement in the events of retirement, disability, and death? The real burden of a pension system is measured by the value of its benefits, not its current contribution cost. The aggregate value of benefits is the current claim on the output of the economy; it is the value of output which those who participate actively in production turn over to those who are in receipt of pensions. In this sense, fully advance funded plans may be as burdensome as current funded plans. If we assume that pension saving is effective in adding to output, advance funding in contrast to current funding increases the capital stock. A higher capital-to-labor ratio raises real wages but, assuming fixed real replacement rates, it adds to the real value of pensions. If the ratio of covered retired to total population is the same in the two cases, an advance funded system will have the same ratio of pension income to total income as a current funded system. With the current funded system, the ratio of contributions to income will be higher; with the advance funded, the ratio of interest income to total income will be higher. These are incidentals; what matters is that the burden of pensions in the two cases is the same. Although used regularly in measurement of the burden of taxes, this is a crude concept of burden. With respect to taxes, we hold commonly that, of two equal ratios of taxes to income, one achieved through progressive taxation is less burdensome than another achieved through regressive taxation. So I am using burden in a special sense: it is merely the claim of pensions on output.

If we could discover the optimum burden of pensions, we would have a guide to setting wage replacement rates and normal retirement ages. There are several ways that one might approach the problem of determining what the optimum is. An underconsumptionist might argue that supporting the aged, disabled, and survivors is an alternative to imperialism as a means for maintaining markets in a capitalist economy, and that some such thinking must underlie the retirement test. This approach assumes that certain free-market adjustment processes are inoperative and, indeed, they may not function very well, but perhaps we could improve their working. A better approach might be to begin with the recognition that retirement is an exercise of choice with respect to the consumption of leisure. The consumption of lifetime leisure may be bunched all at the end, all at the beginning, or spread rather evenly over the expected life span. To make any progress along this approach, we require a knowledge of people's preferences for the time scheduling of leisure. We can reduce our planning information requirements by simply building into pension design greater flexibility, and then allowing individuals to choose how they will schedule their leisure. Going all the way, we would start everyone off at maturity with a present cash value of subsidized leisure. One could claim it at any rate one wanted, subject only to the constraint that if one became, through unwise choices, a public nuisance, some suitable penalty would be imposed. One would, of course, have a power of appointment over any sum remaining at one's death.

Intriguing as this suggestion may be, we will not go all the way, at least in OASDI. An essential element in OASDI is compulsory provision for retirement, disability, and death, and there is no indication that we are prepared to abandon that principle. We could, however, in employee plans, gather up vacation time, sick leave, severance pay, retirement, disability, and survivorship into a single program of compensated nonwork. To deal with spendthrifts, we could restrict the amount of paid leisure a worker could take in any year to some fraction of the amount becoming available that year, and maintain that rule until such time as the worker became really disabled or attained some advanced age, at which time that individual could take paid leave at a faster rate. Under this scheme, employees could bargain with their employer for goods versus paid leisure just as they now do. Choosing less paid leisure, their employer's output would be greater and their wages higher. Choosing more leisure, their employer's output would be less and their wages lower.

6. **Even though we do not know the optimum pension burden and are not agreed on wage-replacement rates, the projections in recent trustees reports suggest that the time has come to reconsider normal retirement age.** The time has come for both employee plans and OASDI, although for somewhat different reasons. Employee plans should be concerned about possible lengthening mean life. OASI has not only that to worry about but the effect of retirement on the labor force. Retirement under an employee plan requires that a worker leave the firm or the industry but ordinarily not the labor force. The OASI retirement test does require substantial retirement from the labor force. The effect of the OASI retirement test is to encourage the substitution of home work for market work and, to the extent that it does, it introduces inefficiencies into the utilization of labor that we may not want for the future. From another standpoint, that of the optimum allocation of income over a lifetime, early retirement under employee plans may not be in the public interest or indeed even in private interests. This is the case when plans take away dollars of a current marginal utility substantially higher than the current marginal utility of the dollars that they pay back. For workers with good earning opportunities following retirement from their primary employment, current employee plans may do just that.

We might consider moving the OASI normal retirement age toward age 70 and abandoning the retirement test. The federal government might reconsider its own employee plan practices with respect both to civil and military retirement. But tax subsidies extended to any employee plans should be withdrawn at the point where those plans seem to be reallocating lifetime income in an uneconomic way. This is not an easy test to apply. The whole point of OASDI is to tax away dollars that at time t have a high value, and pay back dollars which at time *t* have a low value. Everything depends upon how contributors and grant recipients view the program. And there are some accommodations that can be made. Younger workers not satisfied with paying the contributions probably can shift them partially through wage bargains with employers.

7. **Efforts should be made to improve disability insurance and unemployment insurance programs—government and private—so that retirement programs are used less to compensate for the inadequacies of disability and unemployment programs.** What perhaps should be regarded as an alarming proportion of workers under OASDI choose early retirement and, since many workers under employee plans are eligible for even earlier retirement, a higher proportion of retirees each year under employee plans may not have attained age 65. Early retirement seems to be associated in good part with the disabilities and the difficulties of securing or keeping full-time work that come with aging. Of course, it is well that workers unable to work have something to fall back upon, but the substitution of retirement grants for disability and unemployment program treatments is unfortunate. By making it possible for older people to live without working, we encourage them to leave the paid labor force prematurely. Provided with physical and psychological rehabilitation, retraining, and relocation, in addition to cash grants that tide them over a transition, many workers would choose to remain active to a later age. Keeping them in the paid labor force until normal retirement age, we would have their product; they would have higher incomes and retire on full pensions.

Improving disability and unemployment insurance programs presents a difficulty that is of increasing concern. Until this difficulty is resolved, there will be some opposition to improving and extending disability and unemployment programs. The difficulty is that, apparently on an argument that disability and unemployment grants are analogous to life insurance proceeds, they have been exempt from federal income tax. Thus, given a choice between equal disability and retirement pensions, a person naturally chooses the disability pension, and earnings must be significantly above unemployment grants to induce a person to return to work. This difficulty, like many that we have, is an instance of legal analogies ignoring economic realities. Response to the mistake has been truly remarkable. There are two ways out. We could adopt more restrictive definitions of disability and unemployment, but this would shift even more people onto the retirement programs. The other and preferable way is legislation requiring inclusion of disability and unemployment grants in income for federal income tax.

8. **With the maturing of OASDI and employee pension plans, we should begin reducing the differentials in federal income tax treatments of collective and personal lifetime income averaging and the discrimination against personal saving in general.** In the Pension Reform Act of 1974 the Congress adopted certain limits on the amount of benefits which pension plans could provide. For defined benefit plans the limit is $75,000 or 100 percent of high three-year average income. The limitations evidently reflect a view that there is some rate or level of wage replacement beyond which the public interest is negligible and the federal income tax treatment of pension plan saving should be similar to the treatment of personal saving. Under the enacted rules, a differential in favor of pension saving remains because there is no requirement for the inclusion in income of current interest earnings on the excess pension saving. The provisions in the legislation relating to personal retirement saving merely reduce the discrimination against personal saving for the specific objective of providing retirement income. But inconsistency in the treatment of saving is the major defect in the federal income tax. We have two routes to reform: include in the tax base all saving on an accrual accounting and tax it at uniform rates, or exclude all saving from the tax base. I here support a comprehensive accrual inclusion, but the alternative is attractive.

But it is the discrimination against personal saving—whatever its objective—that is difficult to justify now that it is unlikely that a general differential in favor of pension saving will induce substantial additional growth in employee pension plan coverage. By some rule that truly reflects the public interest in pension plan saving, some part of employer contributions to plans and the interest earnings on those funds should be includible in the incomes of employees for purposes of computing federal income tax liabilities. At the very least, the rule should apply to contributions made for employees having vested rights. The argument that the employer contribution is not income under a general realization concept is not correct. In fact the employee enjoyed during the year something of value, the promise that he will receive a pension when and if certain conditions are satisfied. In principle, employer contributions to pension plans should be included in income for the same reason that deductions from income are not allowed for life insurance premia; in both cases there is a consumer outlay on a service enjoyed during the premium or contribution period. Furthermore, taxing employer contributions to employees with and without vested rights is the single most effective way we have of promoting early vesting and, at the same time, restraining the substitution of current money wages for other plan "improvements." Attributing employer contributions to employee income, we could also restrain overfunding of plans. Certainly no public purpose is served in funding to the point where fund earnings will pay pensions entirely, nor should there be a financial incentive, as there is now, for a company to use a pension fund as a device for avoiding the accumulated earnings tax.

With respect to disability programs, both the disability coverage in OASDI and employee plans, we have a choice: tax to employees employer plan contributions when made, or tax the grants when received. That contributions to disability insurance programs should be made out of employee after-tax income is consistent with federal income tax life insurance rules. Although, in permitting employers to pay life insurance premia without attribution to employees, the federal income tax treatment is not internally consistent, there is a provision that requires attribution to employee income of employer contributions which purchase coverage in excess of $50,000. While, in principle, it would be better to tax the contributions, often there are no contributions, the disability grants being treated as employer current costs. For administrative reasons it may be better to tax the grants when received.

For OASI, the rule should be the same as for employee plans, with the exception that the implicit interest on OASI contributions cannot be known until the employee is in retirement. One solution is to require that OASI beneficiaries include in income for tax the difference between their annual grants and an appropriate fraction of their employers' and their own total contributions. Doing this, we would require, as under employee plans, that employer contributions be included in income when made. This supposes that we want to retain payroll tax financing of OASI. As compared to federal personal income tax financing of OASI, the FICA tax is not a good tax. Because we cannot assume that the supply of labor is independent of its price, some part of the employee tax and of the employer tax must be shifted forward through higher prices. I would guess that nearly all of the employer tax is shifted forward, and that most of the employee tax is accepted by workers as a reasonable price to pay for the OASI grants promised. Nevertheless, any forward shifting involves a distortion in worker choices of market versus home work, and in relative prices of output. The welfare loss from forward shifting of employer and employee taxes may be substantial. Abolishing the employer tax, we could maintain individual social security accounts, and families wanting coverage for a member not in the paid labor force could buy it by paying an additional FICA tax. Of course, by abolishing both FICA taxes and financing OASI grants from general revenues or just the federal personal income tax, we could avoid the expense of account-keeping and base grants on wage income reported on tax returns for a few years prior to retirement.

Chapter 5

An Economic Theory of the Social Security System and Its Relation to Fiscal Policy

James N. Morgan

The social security system in the United States has been called social insurance, a compact between generations, a mechanism for income redistribution, and an insurance and welfare system; it is in part all of these things. Some have focused on the insurance aspects and insisted that every detail fit that model, ignoring other important and justifiable purposes of the system. More recently, the intergenerational aspects have come into question as people argue that the compact is not fair when a smaller younger generation must be taxed to pay benefits for a larger older generation. It is this issue we want to focus on first. We shall argue that the notion of an intergenerational compact has been misleading, that at least after the initial generation that was brought in early, each generation can and should be treated as "paying its own way." Indeed, from such a notion we can derive some rules about the proper level of social security taxes and benefits and the proper use of general tax funds in paying social security retirement benefits. First, let us back off and look realistically at how any economy does in fact provide for its current nonproductive members.

We shall not discuss children and dependents who are largely taken care of inside the family or with different income-maintenance programs, nor the insurance-like parts of the social security system. We focus on retirement benefits. We must distinguish the real production, consumption, and capital formation implications of the system from the money transactions and legal arrangements. And we must distinguish the social security taxes and benefits of each generation from the fiscal aspects of how the current surpluses or deficits are handled. Finally, we must also be careful in going from consideration of an individual to talking about a whole cohort, because most of the redistribution *between* generations is unintended and likely to be considered inequitable. We start with the individual.

Individuals have earning lives during which they can expect to consume much of their earned income in taking care of the current needs of themselves and their dependents, both through direct payments and indirectly through taxes that pay for government services. The residual that is not consumed or paid in taxes either provides or could provide a retirement fund, which, properly invested, should earn a real rate of return of around 3 percent. When there is inflation, it should earn the market rate, the difference being roughly equal to the rate of inflation.[1] Given a working life and an expected retirement age and lifetime, we know how much retirement annuity such saving would provide in real terms, relative to preretirement income. (See appendix for illustrative tables.)

How do we interpret and analyze a system where some part of that saving is represented by social security taxes? We argue that in discussing the theory and justification of the system, and even for discussing the proper amount of social security taxes and retirement benefits, we should temporarily ignore the money-flow aspects of the system and think only of its real implications.

If the age group in question had spent the money instead of paying the social security taxes, the national level of investment would have suffered unless someone had been induced to save and invest in some other way.[2] The real saving represented by the social security taxes allowed someone, somewhere, the opportunity to use those resources for productive investment. That investment should have produced a return of 3 percent in real terms, or at market rates in money terms. It is not, of course, a matter of indifference whether the government actually invests the accumulated funds. In fact, because of fiscal policy considerations or a desire to provide benefits for a previous generation that grew up before the social security system started, the government spent much of them and put the system on a pay-as-you-go basis. The fact that since then each generation of workers has paid its social security taxes, and hence consumed less, gives it a right to a fair return, both interest and principal, on those

1. This has been true historically, but its logical base is the assumption that the real return on capital investment is 3 percent per year on the average.

2. We don't argue that Social Security taxes (plus the promise of benefits) reduced only spending; they might have come partly out of other savings. It is the justification of a return on the accumulated Social Security taxes that concerns us.

savings. *That return should both justify and set the amount of their retirement payments.* If they had saved the money privately, or even in a properly run private pension plan, we would expect the same benefits, and we might blame the individual or the employer if the trusteeship of the fund was inadequate and it did not earn its 3 percent in real terms. However, earning a market interest rate that also offsets inflation might be difficult for a private pension scheme.

The social security system's prior and main obligation is to pay to each generation of workers benefits that reflect their taxes plus an adequate rate of return on the accumulated savings. Of course, the "fund" must also stay "solvent" in a current liquidity sense. If the current tax payments of a smaller working generation will not cover the retirement annuities of a larger previous generation, this is not a crisis but a liquidity problem. There is no reason why the aggregate tax payments of one generation would pay for the aggregate benefit payments of another generation, even if one added interest. The amount paid to retired age groups should depend on what they paid in, plus a reasonable accumulation of interest that could have been earned if those funds had been invested elsewhere in the economy. The still-working cohort should pay an amount in social security taxes that, if it earned market interest rates, would provide for its own retirement benefits later.[3]

If these criteria for determining social security taxes and benefits leave the current flow out of balance so that the pay-as-you-go system does not seem to work, the balance should not be achieved by changing social security taxes or benefits, since that would merely make things worse. Hopefully the capital investment that past nonconsuming due to social security taxes allowed has increased productivity of both labor and capital, hence there is justification for using federal income taxes, personal and corporate, to provide that interest return on the "investment." We defer to public finance specialists as to the optimal mix of taxes for the purpose.

The size of the social security trust fund, on which interest is paid

3. We are excluding from consideration in this discussion all other aspects of the system—survivors', disability, and medical benefits—not because they are not a substantial element, but to keep the analysis simple. They lead to substantial redistribution among the members of the same generation, from those who work many years and have no troubles, to the survivors of those who die, to the disabled and the ill, to those who worked somewhat fewer years or at low wages. These redistributions, whether income-based or incident-based, can be considered as happening within each age group and are important in calculating equity since the ratio of Social Security taxes to retirement benefits alone, ignoring these other benefits, can be badly misleading. Asking about special subgroups such as those who die early without survivors and never collect benefits belongs in the discussion of redistribution rather than retirement annuities.

(not earned in any real sense), has no systematic relationship to the imaginary fund that could be built up from the savings of each generation, and which presumably could be invested so as to produce a real (3 percent) return to add to the savings, and produce an adequate retirement income.

It was clear when the social security system began that it would be impossible to accumulate all the savings until the first age groups could qualify to start collecting benefits, since the government could not invest the funds in real capital and equipment that would pay a return, and if they were simply hoarded, the fiscal consequences would be devastatingly depressive. Indeed, bringing in a group who had not been paying for very long and giving them retirement benefits was partly an act of mercy, but partly a way of avoiding fiscal side-effects during a depression when there was need for more consumption before anyone could justify more investment.

The current concern that outpayments may exceed social security taxes because of the differing sizes of succeeding generations, and a technical error in the inflation adjustment built into the system, is merely another part of this same old problem. A private company can put its employees' pension fund into productive investments, but the government is limited to investing in nonproductive government obligations and has the additional concern about the aggregate fiscal impact.[4]

How could the government see to it that there was sufficient investment somewhere to represent the investment of an imaginary savings fund built up of the social security taxes? Perhaps by actually accumulating a fund and encouraging private investment sufficient to offset the spending deficiency that would otherwise occur? A re-reading of the literature at the time the system began will surely reveal that we expected the system to get in balance so that, although each generation built up a huge fund, the total fund could stabilize as the outpayments of retired generations equaled the inpayments of current workers, plus interest earned.

It is interesting to note that the original discussions of the relative reliance on employer contributions, employee contributions, and government contribution (ignoring whether seen as interest on a trust fund), justified the 30 percent, 30 percent, and 40 percent, respectively, on the ground that the 40 percent government contribution

4. One could, of course, preserve appearances by putting the funds in special government bonds that paid market interest rates. But the interest still comes out of taxes. For a thorough discussion of the possible effects of the Social Security program on saving and ways of integrating the program with fiscal policy, see Lesnoy and Hambor (1975) and Feldstein (1974). For a classic study of the effects of private pensions on saving, see Katona (1965).

was the cost of providing retirement benefits for several initial generations who had not contributed very much to the system.

In fact, in an inflation-free world, the 3 percent real return assumption combined with a reasonable expectation of 40 years of contributions and 15 years of retirement would lead to a ratio of total contribution to total pension benefits of 40 percent, less than the 30 + 30 = 60 percent, If there were inflation, meaning a higher market interest rate on the accumulated saving, the ratio of dollar benefits to more valuable dollar contributions would be still larger. For instance, if we can expect 6 percent average market interest rates, then the aggregate contribution over 40 years need only aggregate to 17 percent of the aggregate pension. What we argue is that the rest is legitimately a claim on society by that generation for a fair return on its saving and should be paid out of taxes on all earned income (including interest and dividends), and not regarded as any unjust burden of one generation on another. And the fraction of the pensions that should come out of surrogate interest (general taxes) is clearly very sensitive to the rate of inflation and the interest rate.

But a basic problem remains—where is the real investment that justifies and provides for the 3 percent real rate of return on the real or imaginary fund of savings represented by the accumulated social security taxes of each generation? And if the saving merely allows others to invest without inflation, how do we reestablish the right of the social security system to that return?

Indeed, we can argue that investment increases the returns to all the factors of production, and hence those who saved through the social security system have an economic right to tax all earned incomes for an amount representing a fair return on their savings. This provides both a justification and a key to the amount. If we can accept the notion that investments should earn market interest rates, reflecting both real productivity gains and the impact of inflation, and if we accept the generalization that historically this has meant about a 3 percent rate of return in real terms, then we can state in advance what the social security benefits will be in real terms. The justification for inflation adjustment is also incorporated into the logic, on the basis of economics, not ethics.

Obviously some complex actuarial calculations must be made to set tax rates, and they are complicated by the fact that part of the social security taxes go to pay for survivors' benefits, disability benefits, and Medicare, which are more heavily redistributive and have a different time pattern than retirement benefits. Also, those who die before retirement provide for some of the redistributive benefits, unless one wants to complicate the annuity calculations further.

If we can explain, rationalize, and justify the taxes and benefits of each generation on an argument that their taxes plus a real 3 percent return pay for that generation's benefits, and if we can explain why that justifies taxes on all earned incomes to make up the difference between aggregate social security taxes and aggregate benefits, we are still left with two problems. First, there is the fiscal impact of the system, since it is the government receipts and expenditures that affect the level of the economy; and second, there are implications for the optimal level of national investment.

We shall not go into the first of these, which has been extensively discussed from the beginning, except to note that discussions of the size of the trust fund and the rate of interest credited to it have little to do with the basic logic of the social security system we have been discussing.

The more interesting and difficult question is what the analysis of the system tells us about the optimum level of aggregate investment, and about the interpretation of the rights to the return on that investment. If the government accumulated no fund, then while a partial equilibrium analysis might argue that the lower consumption of workers paying the social security tax "allowed" more investment without inflation, in fact someone else had to save to offset the government's spending of those taxes currently, and those people would have the apparent legal right to the return on those investments. Worse still, there is no mechanism to assure that total investment will even reflect the amount of saving done by workers through their social security taxes. The system started in a period when we had the classic Keynesian problem of inadequate total demand, and fiscal policy called for more consumption first, before more investment could be expected to come along. Current claims that we have a deficiency of investment may be correct, but there is no easy way to use the social security system to assure it. Building up a larger trust fund invested in government securities would not do it except very indirectly by depressing interest rates, and would have to be done by general taxes rather than by social security tax hikes if we are to accept the notion that each generation would "pay its own way."[5]

Perhaps we can argue that at a minimum there should be at least enough investment to reflect replacement of the capital stock and to increase it by the amount an imaginary trust fund would increase if

5. And if we worry that Social Security taxes (plus promised benefits) discourage other saving, we could equally worry that investment of any retirement fund might discourage other investment. We may well have to have a flexible national policy striving to end up with an optimal investment level, whatever the effects of social insurance.

all the social security taxes plus a 3 percent real interest rate were put in trust.

On the other hand, except for short-run differences offset by government surpluses or deficits, aggregate investment should also equal aggregate private saving. Perhaps, we now have a policy implication that whether the government should be stimulating private investment or achieving fiscal balance through fiscal policy depends partly on whether investment threatens to be below our theoretical minimum.

Actually, when the social security system is in some kind of balance, the aggregate size of the imaginary ("fully funded") trust fund (including interest) should not change much except as the sizes of succeeding generations differ. The requirement that it "earn" market interest rates to reflect both real productivity and inflation merely justifies increased dollar taxes to supplement the current social security taxes in meeting the current payments of the system.

We are left with the feeling that except as a cushion there is no need for a trust fund, and its fluctuating size has little real meaning. We have argued that the proper level of social security taxes should be set on the basis of societally determined levels of real benefits, and their actuarial cost assuming a real 3 percent rate of return on postponed consumption. In this sense each generation pays its own way, and the redistributional aspects of the system are largely intragenerational. We have argued that the return on the delayed consumption of workers should be paid for out of taxes on all earned income since, at least in a partial equilibrium sense, it was the lowered consumption of workers that should have allowed the investment that increased earned incomes. We have also suggested that although the notion of "allowed investment" might seem to set some minimum limits on aggregate investment, the latter is also required to balance voluntary private saving, and in any case, the aggregate size of the imaginary social security fund will not change much as the "dissaving" of retired workers of one generation balances the "saving" of current workers.

What are the implications of the requirement that the implicit accumulation of savings of each generation earn market interest rates? The impact of inflation is to require heavier future taxes on all earned incomes to pay the higher dollar benefits; but these higher taxes are not an unwarranted burden on working generations to help the older retired generations, they are merely part of the impact of inflation. So a global consideration of the social security system makes us look at the consequences of inflation more carefully, just as we are encouraged to reexamine our notions of optimal aggregate investment. While it is true that there was a technical error in the recent automatic inflation adjustment written into the social security system, the general principle of indexing benefits is not only appropriate, but should not be considered as charity, nor as intergenerational transfers, but as a legitimate application of market interest to the accumulated postponed consumption of each generation.

INTRAGENERATIONAL EQUITY

We have been focusing exclusively on intergenerational equity, and on the appropriate pattern of overall taxes and benefits for each generation. The issue of equity *within* any one age group has been widely discussed and, in the case of women, well-treated in a recent Senate Committee Print (U.S. Senate, 1975).

We shall not go over all this ground, except to argue in general that much of the rhetoric ignores basic economic considerations. Indeed, while there are a number of substantial improvements that should be made relating to the treatment of *some* women under social security, overall they benefit more now than men do from most of the *intra*-generational redistribution aspects of the system, as Robert M. Ball, former commissioner, testified:

> On an overall basis women workers as a group in comparison to men as a group do well under the American Social Security system. There are changes that should be made, both to improve the protection that women have under the program and to remove the last vestiges of different treatment based upon sex, but it is not correct to argue for these changes on the ground that women workers as a group get less for their contributions than do men workers as a group. Actually, the cost arising from women-workers' accounts and male-workers' accounts is approximately the same, slightly higher for female workers than for male workers. This is true because the longer life expectancy of women, the fact that fewer of them work beyond 65, and the fact that as a group they receive a greater advantage from the weighted benefit formula in relation to the contributions that they pay, more than makes up for the fact that male-worker accounts generate more secondary beneficiaries, e.g. wife's and widow's benefits. [U.S. Senate, 1975, pp. 16–17.]

There is, of course, no intrinsic reason why the system should not end up benefiting women *substantially* more than men. There is a problem, however, that some complaints by women deal with life situations where an *individual* gets out considerably less than he or she puts in (usually because that person is relatively well off or dies and does not need it). Applying that kind of justification for change would lead to much larger changes in favor of unmarried workers without dependents (mostly males). It amounts to eliminating some of the redistributive mechanisms that were purposely put into the system.

There must be a basic reconciliation within each generation between a desire for applying insurance and annuity principles on the one hand, and providing for some redistribution on the other. If each generation is to pay its own way as suggested in the first part of this paper, then improved benefits for one subgroup mean lower benefits or higher taxes for others.[6]

In particular, the income test for retirement benefits was justified originally by the argument that people who can still work and earn do not need the retirement benefits. If we are to regard this provision as an unwarranted redistribution, we would have to increase the taxes or decrease the benefits of those who do not work after 65, in order to provide benefits for those who do, mostly a redistribution from lower-income to higher-income people. Indeed, a stronger argument can be made for counting all taxable income in the test, although such a rule could be easily avoided by transferring property into trusts or giving it to children early.

There is another sense in which the income test might be considered inequitable, and that is where the income is earned serving community needs doing things for which the market cannot provide competitive wages. We now give people a choice between doing such work for nothing or taking pay and losing some of their social security benefits. We might, for example, define a class of jobs—serving community needs, unable to pay full wages—and a class of people (those over 65 and receiving social security benefits) for which the income test would not apply if some pay were given for that work and this income might even be exempt from federal income taxes, at least at lower incomes. This would encourage older people to participate and allow them to earn without providing benefits for nonretired workers in excellent economic condition and without encouraging older people to do philanthropic work for nothing when they could be paid at least something for it. It would not be seen as taking jobs from younger workers. New opportunities would open up without bringing in a whole new bureaucracy of administrators and program directors.

Another change in society that may lead to greater inequities in the future is that we may have more men and women who work less

6. But discussions of impact must consider the Social Security taxes and benefits together. It is not useful to discuss the "regressivity of the Social Security tax" separately from the progressivity of the benefits.

than their whole working life within the social security system. The extreme example is the person who qualifies for a pension from a government job, then works long enough also to qualify for social security. We did not worry about this with women, many of whom did not use their benefits because they could get more as dependents of a husband. But a whole generation is coming along that is very late getting social security covered work, in some cases works irregularly, but gets into the covered labor force in time to qualify for benefits. How will we feel about redistribution in their favor out of contributions of others who have contributed for a full working life? Actually, the system requires a longer and longer period of contributions to qualify, and the number of years that can be dropped out in computing averages is small, but the principle and the problem remain. Using such a long period exacerbates the problem of income increases that come late in the earning life. They call for special added saving to restrict the increase in level of consumption and to provide for that increment after retirement. To provide for the increased benefits without the added contribution, as some private pension plans do, is inequitable between people with different income patterns and makes estimation of the future pension obligation aggregates difficult. It should, however, be possible to allow and encourage voluntary supplement payments into a fund for this purpose and, if it were done through social security, to guarantee market interest rates on that fund too so that the supplemental pension would also rise with inflation. (See Appendix, especially Table 5–3).

SECULAR CHANGES

A longer term and more basic change comes from the extension of life spans. If a person expects to live longer, then he or she must either retire a little later or save more to provide for a longer retirement. It turns out that under reasonable assumptions, one can "split the gains" evenly. One more year of working life, postponing retirement one year, will provide for one more year of retirement income. The reason is that one added year of work and saving means also one more year of interest accumulation on the whole retirement fund, and a larger fund earning interest over the remaining years as well.

Hence, if expected life spans increase, we shall have to raise social security taxes, or increase the retirement age, or force people to rely even more heavily on supplemental sources of retirement income. There may be superior intermediate options such as stepwise retirement, and as economists we subscribe to the general notion that the more options available the better, provided they are actuarially equivalent and do not burden some people more heavily than others.

Providing more options for people who have retired from their main jobs means more than simply changing laws about income tests for social security, or what is taxable income, or whether the minimum wage law applies. It probably requires the development of organizations and institutional arrangements. The recent explosion of organized encouragement of volunteer work may be an example, but for the aged who are penalized for accepting pay due to the income test, there is not a free choice. It is not at all clear that it is fair to have low-income old people providing free services for the benefit of people with much higher incomes. Organized ways for older people to be paid tax-free and income-test-free compensation for certain socially useful services which the market is incapable of providing could be developed.[7]

Such developments require not rigid experimental designs bound to fail if any important contingency was not foreseen, but monitored developmental experiments with feedback and change built into them and with clear measurable criteria of success. Even when a successful institution seems to have been developed, we may have to retain some of the capacity to change and adapt if attempts to export it to other communities and expand it to other social needs are to succeed.

A basic problem we noticed more than a decade ago when we studied early retirement, and one we are currently hoping to reassess with a study now in the field, is the growing polarity among the aged (Barfield and Morgan, 1974). There are some who retire early—many opted for the 62 retirement as soon as it was allowed—because they were having trouble keeping employed or their health had given out. Many of these had not planned to retire, certainly not early, and were in poor economic circumstances, even with social security. On the other hand, there were others, and we think they may be a growing fraction, who retire early, or on time, because they have accumulated other pension rights in addition to social security, or have accumulated other savings or annuities. They are in grand shape, retire early, and may even be able to cope with inflation. The last ten years have seen increasing unemployment and inflation, but they have also seen high and rising incomes for many. Many of the provisions intended to help the aged, such as double income tax exemptions, benefit mostly the affluent aged, increasing the discrepancy between the two groups of retired.

7. Some would restrict the tax exemption to lower income people, particularly where the social need was not pressing.

This potential polarity, exacerbated by the fact that some have private pension plan coverage and some do not, raises questions of policy. Raising the social security benefits and taxes will not solve the problem, because it would increase the retirement income of the affluent group, too. Encouraging and facilitating extra saving for retirement by those not covered by a second pension plan may well be the best policy. We already have some income tax possibilities, but institutionalization, including even handling of supplemental payments by the social security system, might make it more attractive to workers. Such a voluntary supplemental system would make it easy to do what is optimal, that is, put a larger and larger fraction of each increase in family income into a retirement fund, the later in life the increment comes. (See Appendix, Table 5–3, lower right section.)

SUMMARY

We have argued that a clear conceptual treatment of the social security system based on solid economic analysis requires separating the social insurance aspects from other issues of optimal national investment, and of fiscal and monetary equilibrium. We show that once the level of retirement benefits is fixed, an appropriate level of social security taxes, plus interest on that deferred consumption, can be determined. This in turn will determine current aggregate levels of tax collection and benefit payments. Though this will have fiscal implications, neither the fiscal-monetary impact nor the need to assure the investment required to pay the interest should be an excuse to tinker with the social security retirement system.

Looked at this way, the social security trust fund becomes a liquidity buffer. There is no economic impossibility in providing adequately for our aged, since these are transfers, and in any case we have unemployed resources. But we do need clearer logic to explain and justify the system, and should provide a way of determining how much of the benefits should come from payroll taxes and how much from general revenue. We need some innovations to allow more options, such as supplemental annuities, stepwise or partial retirement, and even tax-free and income-test-free kinds of socially useful work for those of the aged who want to do it. If these options are to be realized, some new organizations or institutions may be required. A recapitulation of the main argument may be useful.

1. We assume that many people would not save for retirement if left to their own initiatives, but that they would demand and society

would provide subsistence for their old age. Hence some compulsion is called for.

2. If we compel people to save for their own old age, we must either provide the program, as in social security, or administer the competing private programs as though they were public utilities, with all the double-accounting and regulatory costs and problems involved.

3. A crucial aspect of retirement programs is coping with inflation. We point out that paying market rates of return on the accumulated fund would do it, though assuring the safety of the fund would be difficult without government operation or help. A fixed return is not a fair return in a volatile economy. And such a rate can be credited to accounts even if no full fund is actually accumulated.

4. Each generation as a group should "pay its own way," so that redistribution, whether on an insurance basis (disability, survivors benefits) or on an equity basis (minimum benefits), is within each generation and can be accounted for and expressed as fractions of totals.

5. There is no need for the government actually to accumulate the savings fund in full, indeed doing so would lead to serious problems of fiscal impact and of potential government control of industry. But the accumulating rights to interest on that deferred consumption has implications for aggregate investment policy. There must be enough investment so that the returns on it can pay the interest in real terms.

6. The fiscal impact of the system should be faced like any other force affecting aggregate flows of consumption, saving, or investment. We have mechanisms for achieving fiscal and monetary equilibrium and do not need to tinker with the social insurance system for those purposes.

7. A final problem, which increases in importance as we use longer and longer periods of earnings to compute benefits, rises from increases in income that come near the end of the working life. Adjusting retirement benefits upward requires relatively larger added contributions per year because there are fewer years of contribution relative to the years of retirement. Such increases in contribution have the added advantage that they restrict the increase in levels of living before retirement. We now have no way for people to set up supplemental retirement provisions except through private individual annuities which are difficult to arrange and to make both safe and inflation-proof. And private supplements can only be made tax-deferred if the individual has no private pension. We suggest provid-

ing for voluntary supplemental annuities through the social security system.

APPENDIX: SOME SIMPLE MATHEMATICS OF RETIREMENT ANNUITIES

We can simplify things by agreeing that we will keep everything in constant dollar terms. Then we need only one interest rate, 3 percent, which represents the real return on capital—higher market rates reflecting price inflation.

And we further simplify things by starting with a constant real stream of earnings which is to provide a constant real stream of retirement benefits. Increments in earnings can be treated as a separate saving-annuity problem—that of saving out of the increment enough to provide an increment in the retirement annuity. The difference is that there is a shorter period of accumulation out of the increment, so a larger fraction of it must be saved. That is what life-cycle theories of saving say.

By looking up two conversion numbers in Table 5–2, we can find the relation between the amount of current saving and the amount of retirement annuity it will provide. The goal, of course, is some ratio of retirement annuity to preretirement consumption, not income, since one need not save for retirement out of one's retirement annuity.

Table 5–1 provides the following:

Years of saving determine: $\dfrac{\text{Accumulated fund (with interest) at end of period of working-saving}}{\text{Amount saved per year}}$

Years of expected retirement life determine: $\dfrac{\text{Annuity payable per year of retirement}}{\text{Accumulated fund at beginning of retirement}}$

Since the two "accumulated funds" are the same amount, the product of these two numbers is the:

$$\frac{\text{Retirement annuity}}{\text{Preretirement annual saving}}$$

And if one can determine what the retirement annuity should be relative to preretirement consumption, simple algebra will determine

Table 5–1. Now and Then at 3 Percent[a]

	$1		$1 Per Year	
X (Years)	Present Value if Only Available after X Years	Future Value in X Years if Available Now	Present Value (Cost) of an Annuity to Last X Years	Value at End of Period of X Years of Accumulation Plus Interest "Value of an Annuity"
1	0.971	1.030	0.971	1.030
5	0.863	1.159	4.580	5.309
10	0.744	1.344	8.530	11.464
15	0.642	1.558	11.938	18.599
20	0.554	1.806	14.877	26.870
25	0.478	2.094	17.413	36.459
30	0.411	2.427	19.600	47.575
35	0.355	2.814	21.487	60.462
40	0.307	3.262	23.115	75.401
45	0.264	3.782	24.519	92.720
50	0.228	4.384	25.730	112.797
	$\frac{1}{(1 + 0.03)^n}$	$(1 + .03)^n$	$\frac{(1 - [1 + i]^{-n})}{i}$	$\frac{([1 + i]^n - 1)}{i}$

[a]If market rate is greater than 3 percent, inflation usually wipes out the difference, so you might double your money sooner; but it would not be double in real purchasing power.

Table 5–2. Ratio of Retirement Income to Preretirement Saving: Retirement Annuity Per Year/Preretirement Annual Saving as a Function of Expected Years of Saving and Years of Retirement *(at 3 percent)*

	Expected Years of Retirement[a]				
Expected Years of Saving	*5*	*10*	*15*	*20*	*25*
5	1.16	0.62	0.44	0.36	0.30
10	2.50	1.34	0.96	0.77	0.66
15	4.06	2.18	1.55	1.25	1.07
20	5.87	3.15	2.25	1.81	1.54
25	7.96	4.27	3.05	2.45	2.09
30	10.39	5.58	3.99	3.19	2.73
35	13.20	7.09	5.06	4.06	3.47
40	16.46	8.84	6.32[b]	5.07	4.33
45	20.24	10.87	7.77	6.23	5.32
50	24.63	13.22	9.45	7.58	6.48

[a] An "optimal" annuity, one-third on the life of each spouse and one-third a joint-or-survivor annuity, where the wife is two years older than the husband, is roughly equivalent in cost to a single-life annuity based on an expected life of 80.

[b] Accumulation = 47.575 × Annual Saving: Table 5–1, column 4.

$$\text{Annuity} = \frac{1}{11.938} \times \text{Accumulation: Table 5–1, column 3.}$$

$$\therefore \text{Annuity/Annual Saving} = \frac{\text{Annuity}}{\text{Accumulation}} \times \frac{\text{Accumulation}}{\text{Annual Saving}}$$

$$= \frac{1}{11.938} \times 45.575 = 6.32.$$

what preretirement saving should be, relative to preretirement consumption or relative to preretirement income.

For example, suppose we assume someone starts working at age 25, retires at 65, and has a life expectancy of 80. This means 40 years of work and saving, and 15 years of retirement.

From Table 5–1, column 4, we see that at 65 the person would have, not 40 times, but 75.4 times his annual saving in a fund.

From Table 5–1, column 3, we see that a lifetime annuity could be purchased for less than 15 times the annual amount even though the average annuitant would live that long, because the remaining fund earns interest. So the annual annuity would be 1/11.9 of the initial fund or price, not 1/15.

The product of accumulation/saving and annuity/accumulation is equal to the annuity/saving both in annual terms: 75.4 (1/11.9) =

6.32; $100 a month saved will provide a retirement annuity of $632 a month.

Table 5–2 gives the range of such feasible annuities. It illustrates the substantial importance of interest accumulation, even at the low 3 percent rate, when long periods of time are involved. The first year of savings in a 40-year working life earns interest for 40 years until retirement, more than tripling its value (Table 5–1, column 2), and then continues to earn until it is finally spent. Starting in the upper left corner of Table 5–2 and going down diagonally to the right are the cells where one is saving for as many years as the number of years of retirement consumption. If the saving were "in a mattress," the annuity per year or month would be identical with the amount saved per year, or month. In the upper left cell, where only ten years altogether are involved, the actual annuity is only 16 percent higher than the no-interest base; but with 25 years of accumulation and 25 years of consumption of a fund, the pension is twice the saving rate (2.09).

If we can set a goal in terms of the ratio of retirement annuity to preretirement income, we can derive the required ratio of preretirement saving to preretirement income. But sensible goals relate retirement income to preretirement consumption (income minus saving for retirement). A little algebra will show that the required ratio of saving to income is equal to:

$$\frac{\text{Ratio of desired annuity to preretirement consumption } (= D)}{\begin{array}{l}\text{Ratio of desired annuity to}\\ \text{preretirement consumption}\end{array} + \begin{array}{l}\text{Potential annuity as ratio}\\ \text{of actual saving } (= K)\end{array}}$$

Because:

$$\text{Annuity}/(\text{Income-Saving}) = D = \text{a goal}$$

$$\text{Annuity}/\text{Saving} = K = \text{a fact, given expected years of work and retirement}$$

So:

$$\text{Annuity} = D\ (\text{Income}) - D\ (\text{Saving})$$

$$\text{Annuity} = K\ (\text{Saving})$$

So:

$$K\ (\text{Saving} = D\ (\text{Income}) - D\ (\text{Saving})$$

$$D\ (\text{Income} = \text{Saving}\ (D + K)$$

$$\text{Saving}/\text{Income} = D/(D + K)$$

Table 5–3 gives examples of the required ratios of saving to income to produce desired ratios of retirement annuity to preretirement consumption (income minus saving for retirement). Reducing the ratio of preretirement consumption one wants to maintain, at least down to 70 percent, has far less effect than changing the age of retirement (which reduces years of saving and interest accumulation *and* increases years of retirement).

The bottom part of Table 5–3 shows how an increasing fraction of *increments of income* must be saved, the later in life the pay raise comes. It is here where relating desired annuity to preretirement consumption, not income, matters. Otherwise one might call for saving more than all of an increase in income![8]

The sensitivity of required social security taxes to assumptions about working life, age of retirement, and norms for adequacy of levels of retirement income is obvious from the tables, and suggests that conclusions about equity and required taxes will require simulation studies. Even an assessment of the current tax and benefit package in terms of the basic justification at 3 percent real interest, requires complex calculations beyond the capacity of this author. Perhaps they have been done, but some of the simpler results desperately need to be more broadly reported, and the public needs to be educated as to the real economics of the system, not pseudo-justifications.

References on page 126

8. Ignoring interest, it is easy to see what spreading an increase in income over a remaining lifetime means. If you had ten more years to work, and expected ten years of retirement, saving half of an income increase would accumulate in the first ten years enough to keep up the added spending for the next ten. And if you had five years of extra earnings, but ten years of retirement, saving two-thirds of the increase would do it. The required saving fractions in Table 3 are lower only because of interest accumulated.

Table 5–3. Required Saving Ratios as a Function of Years of Work and Retirement, and Desired Ratio of Retirement Annuity to Preretirement Income—Minus Savings

Expectations				*Ratio of Annual Annuity to Annual Saving*[a]	*Required Saving/Income Ratio*			
				(From Table 5–2):	*Desired Ratio of Retirement Annuity to Preretirement (Income-Saving) => 1.00*[b]			
Work Life	*Retired Life*	*Start at Age*	*Retire at Age*	$\frac{A}{S} = K$	*1.00*	*.90*	*.80*	*.70*
50	5	25	75	24.13	.04	.04	.03	.03
45	10	25	70	10.87	.08	.08	.07	.06
40	15	25	65	6.32	.14	.12	.11	.10
35	20	25	60	4.06	.20	.18	.16	.11
30	25	25	55	2.73	.27	.25	.23	.20
40	15	25	65	6.32	.14	.12	.11	.10
35	15	30	65	5.06	.16	.15	.14	.12
30	15	35	65	3.99	.20	.18	.17	.15
25	15	40	65	3.05	.25	.23	.21	.19
20	15	45	65	2.25	.31	.29	.26	.24
15	15	50	65	1.55	.39	.37	.34	.31
10	15	55	65	.96	.51	.48	.45	.42
5	15	60	65	.44	.69	.67	.65	.61

Table reads: Bottom row, third column—if you want to have a retirement income equal to 80 percent of preretirement consumption (income-saving), and plan to retire at 65, you must save 65 percent of a salary increase that starts when you are 60.

[a]Depends on working life and retirement life, both of which depend on life expectancy, expected age of retirement, and age of starting.

[b]Less than 1.00 because of lower income taxes, cessation of work-related expenses, more time to do it yourself, etc.

If: $\frac{\text{Annuity}}{\text{Saving}} = K$ and: Desired $\frac{\text{Annuity}}{\text{Income-Saving}} = D$ then: $\frac{\text{Required Saving}}{\text{Income}} = \frac{D}{D-K}$

[c]Here the table gives fractions of the increment in income that must be saved.

REFERENCES

Barfield, Richard E., and James N. Morgan (1974) *Early Retirement: The Decision and the Experience, and a Second Look.* Survey Research Center, University of Michigan.

Cagan, Philip (1965). *The Effect of Pension Plans on Aggregate Saving* Occasional Paper 95. New York: National Bureau of Economic Research. (Consumers Union Data.)

Feldstein, Martin (1974). "Social Security, Induced Retirement and Aggregate Capital Accumulation," *Journal of Political Economy* 82 (September–October): 905–26.

Katona, George (1965). *Private Pensions and Individual Saving.* Survey Research Center, University of Michigan.

Lesnoy, S.D., and J.C. Hambor (1975). "Social Security, Saving and Capital Formation," *Social Security Bulletin* 38 (July): 3–15.

U.S. Senate (1975). Special Committee on Aging. Task Force on Women and Social Security. *Women and Social Security: Adapting to a New Era.* Washington, D.C.: Government Printing Office.

Comment on Morgan

Charles D. Hobbs

At first reading James Morgan's paper does not appear to be about social security at all, even though he says it is. By simplifying some aspects of social security and disregarding others, he manages to present an idealized national social insurance program so clean and engaging that one is tempted to think we could do worse than to adopt it.

Of course, we *have* done worse. The 40-year-old social security program is threatened with insolvency and looks like a lump of unwashed coal next to Morgan's cleanly faceted diamond. Yet just as coal and diamond are varying forms of the element carbon, so social security and Morgan's idealization are varying forms of the concept of social insurance. And since Morgan purports to be describing and analyzing social security, we must look carefully not only at the differences between his idealization and social security's reality, but also at the potential for realization of his idealized form of social security.

Can a social insurance program be as pristine, fair, and beneficial as Morgan describes it? Before answering that question it is necessary to examine how and why Morgan's description differs from the reality of social security.

First, Morgan strips away the elements of the social security program he considers extraneous to his analysis. To "keep the analysis simple," he excludes survivors' benefits, disability insurance (DI), health insurance (HI), and supplemental medical insurance (SMI), although the benefits of these elements are funded by a formula distribution of the overall social security tax—a tax which originally was levied only to provide a "floor of protection" to the incomes of retired workers. In 1974, DI, HI, and SMI accounted for more than 25 percent of total social security benefit payments and, since social security is essentially a cash-flow operation, for an equivalent portion of social security taxes (Myers, 1975, pp. 392–94).

Since these elements were not part of the original social security program, and since they now constitute one-quarter of it, to remove them from an economic analysis of tax-benefit relationships is to divorce the analysis from the realities of social security.

Second, Morgan posits a social insurance retirement program affected only by demographic fluctuations and inflation. He ignores the leap-frogging real growth of both taxes and benefits which Social Security has experienced. Between 1940 and 1970 the national CPI grew by 147 percent, maximum social security benefits by 305 percent, and maximum social security taxes by 1,544 percent (Hobbs and Powlesland, 1975, p. 5). In virtually every election year since 1950 benefits and the benefit population have been expanded, forcing increases in taxes. Far from being the stable, prudently managed retirement program Morgan describes, social security is a fiscally unstable program which has been constantly buffeted by political winds.

Third, Morgan attempts to wish away the effects of inflation on social security by assuming that both the tax receipts of the program and the additional retirement investments of workers will earn at a "market rate" of the rate of inflation plus 3 percent. He ignores the disproportionately adverse effects of inflation on low- and middle-income workers and retirees. Savings accounts and insurance policies seldom provide a return of the inflation rate plus 3 percent. The returns on such investments—usually the only ones available to low- and middle-income people—often do not even match the inflation rate. Moreover, as wages rise to meet inflation, the percentage of earned income taken by the income tax rises, reducing the percentage of income which can be invested even in savings accounts and insurance policies. The combination of inflation, a progressive income tax, and constantly rising social security taxes has effectively removed from low- and middle-income families the opportunity to save for their own retirement, a fact which Morgan excludes from his analysis.

These differences between Morgan's description and the actual social security program become analytical deficiencies when he attempts to draw conclusions about social security. He argues that the "notion of an intergenerational compact has been misleading," and that "after the initial generation that was brought in early, each generation is to be treated as 'paying its own way.' " Thus, "if the current tax payments of a smaller working generation will not cover the retirement annuities of a larger previous generation, this is not a crisis but a liquidity problem," which he would solve though the temporary infusion of general funds into social security. But the fiscal impact of differences in the populations of successive generations is small compared to the deficits produced by legislatively created expansions of benefits and eligibility. The present fiscal dilemma is politically, not demographically, based.

Congress fears that American workers will not tolerate further social security taxes to fund already promised benefits. The use of general funds to correct the imbalance is politically appealing because the tax effects would not be felt by the people for several years. During those years Congress would be free to continue its past policy of overpromising and overspending. The temporary infusion of general funds would become a permanent component of social security revenues—a double tax on workers who even now cannot look forward to getting as much out of social security as they will have put into it by the time they retire.

Morgan goes on to say that "a re-reading of the literature at the time the system began will surely reveal that we expected the system to get in balance so that, although each generation built up a huge fund, the total fund could stabilize as the outpayments of retired generations equaled the inpayments of current workers plus interest earned." Unfortunately, the re-reading Morgan suggests does not support his contention. Edwin Witte, chairman of Franklin Roosevelt's Committee on Economic Security, which formulated the social security program and its legislation, has stated that the committee "was told by its staff that the taxes currently collected would not meet the costs of benefits after 1965" (Witte, 1962, p. 148). When Roosevelt realized that the program was designed to go broke, he required the authors of the legislation to double the original tax rate —from 0.5 percent to 1.0 percent. The actuaries estimated that the increased tax revenues yielded under this plan would enable the old age insurance system to remain entirely self-supporting, *at least until 1980*" (Witte, 1962, p. 151) (emphasis added). These estimates were based on an ever-increasing worker population with no generational fluctuations. The program was not expected to get in balance, even with a double tax rate.

Witte admitted that the Committee on Economic Security "accepted the idea that the deficits resulting thereafter should be met from general tax sources" (p. 148). But that is hardly the same thing as Morgan saying the "the rest (deficit) is legitimately a claim on society by that generation for a fair return on its saving and should be paid out of taxes on all earned income." Witte was describing a deficit produced by the program design; Morgan is attempting to remedy deficits he attributes to population fluctuations between generations. Fluctuations in populations are not the primary cause of the deficit. A poorly designed social security program and an overly generous Congress have caused the current and projected social security deficits. The use of income tax to fund the deficits will only exacerbate the program by encouraging a continuation of past policies.

Morgan's revision of the actual history of social security even extends to the infamous earnings test, by which benefits to a retired worker are decreased proportionate to the amount earned by working beyond normal retirement age. Morgan claims that "the income [sic] test for retirement benefits was justified originally by the argument that people who can still work and earn do not need the retirement benefits." Hardly. When social security was started the national unemployment rate was hovering between 20 and 25 percent, and the earnings test (it is not an "income test" because unearned income is disregarded) was a direct attempt to get the elderly to stop working altogether. For this reason the earnings test does not apply beyond age 72, when it is obvious that a retired worker, after seven to ten years out of the labor market, is no longer much of a competitive threat to younger workers.

The earnings test has had the support of organized labor, especially the AFL–CIO, precisely because it reduces competition in the labor market, although the AFL–CIO attributes its position to the hypocritical nonsense that daily contact with an older worker receiving social security would raise the hackles of his younger co-workers who are paying for it. Such powerful opposition to older workers getting a fair return on their forced investment highlights the question of whether or not an equitable national retirement program can ever be built on the social insurance principles.

One cannot answer this question by revising the unpleasant history or ignoring the inconvenient aspects of social security, as Morgan has done. Social security's excessive costs and individual inequities are not the flaws of an imperfectly developed social insurance program; they are rather the inevitable consequences of any social insurance scheme predicated, as all such schemes are by definition, on the sublimation of individual choice and liberty to the principle of the greatest good for the greatest number. This principle motivated the founders of social security, and has motivated almost all of its apologists and reformers. The effective application of this principle requires a constant redefinition of what is good for society, and in the process of redefinition, costs climb and various groups of individuals are either favored or left behind. The process—carried on by a handful of bureaucrats and legislators—is judgmental, paternalistic, and totally divorced from the idea of equity for any individual.

The economic features of social insurance are centralized wealth redistribution and cash-flow financing, which forces each generation to pay welfare-like benefits to the preceding generation through whatever combination of taxes is established. As Congress manipulates the benefits for political gain, program costs and taxes are virtually certain to rise faster than the cost of living. Rising taxes reduce the private savings and investment potential of the workers, forcing more welfare features into the social insurance program. In the beginning, social security was perceived by the workers to be a pension program, and by its founders to be an insurance program. Now it is obviously more welfare than insurance, more insurance than pension. The trend will continue; federal welfare programs and social security have and will become less and less distinguishable from each other until finally there will be no relationship between social security taxes and benefits.

The final indignity, and the most destructive national effect, of social insurance is the forced reduction in the level of activity of those who retire. Both work and leisure activities are curtailed by social security: investments to supplement benefits have been squeezed off by the high tax rate, those who choose to work find their benefits reduced or cut off entirely, and benefits alone are insufficient for more than subsistence living. The net effect is to decrease the level of economic activity—both getting and spending—among retired workers and their families, and thus to increase the entropy of the entire economy.

Upon reflection, then, it can be seen that James Morgan's paper is doubly deceptive: first because it hides the flaws of social security, and second because it hides the fact that these flaws are inherent in the application of the social insurance concept. Social security reforms based on social insurance principles will further restrict the choices and activities of America's active and retired workers. To solve the problems of social security we must look for alternatives, not embellishments, to the present program.

REFERENCES

Hobbs, Charles D., and Stephen L. Powlesland (1975). *Retirement Security Reform.* Concord, Vermont: Institute for Liberty and Community.

Myers, Robert J. (1975). *Social Security.* Bryn Mawr, Pennsylvania: McCahan Foundation.

Witte, Edwin E. (1962). *The Development of the Social Security Act.* Madison, Wisconsin: University of Wisconsin Press.

 Chapter 6

A Proposal for Reforming the Social Security System

Arthur B. Laffer
R. David Ranson

Morality is an integral part of political economy. Whatever the economics involved, any policy proposal affecting the more vulnerable or the less advantaged members of society that does not address the moral questions explicitly is remiss.

But moral questions are sometimes misperceived. The true moral issue transcends question-begging cliches that are often stated to obtain political gain. Misleading statements are often based on the incorrect view that economic efficiency and morality are inconsistent with one another. Inflating the promises to the disadvantaged often is *less* moral than maintaining restraint. It is an immoral act for a society to promise the undeliverable. It is especially immoral if the people to whom the promises are made are exceptionally vulnerable.

In this proposal, we attempt to provide a correctly conceived moral response to what we perceive as a serious social problem in the United States: namely, the defective constitution of the U.S. social security system and the attendant economic consequences of those defects. As presently constituted, we believe the system will not only *not* deliver its promises but will be *unable* to deliver its promises. Moreover the prospective failure of the social security system is a threat to the health and stability of the entire economy. The challenge today as we see it is to provide an economically sound and efficient system that satisfies society's revealed preference to provide a better life for the aged. Our comments are directed at what we identify as the major shortcomings of the social security system. We do not delve into the numerous detailed problem areas which exist in any complex legislative program. Although the reforms needed are profound, we do not advocate building a new system from scratch. The very existence of our current social security program in itself provides a framework to which millions of people have adapted their lives. It would be counterproductive to dislocate present arrangements in the interest merely of a "clean" theoretical solution to the problem.

A rational and moral proposal for reform of the social security system must satisfy at least two basic objectives. First, the proposal must rid the social security system of its massive unfunded liability. Second, the proposal must eliminate the pronounced and pervasive antiwork biases of the current system. These objectives have to be considered in the context of humanitarian guiding principles.

A failure to satisfy the necessary economic and financial criteria would also be deficient on humanitarian criteria. Only through a technically well-designed system, which explicitly recognizes the possibility of adverse contingencies, can the disadvantaged and uninformed be adequately protected. A system that is constructed with known technical deficiencies such as a massive unfunded liability borders on exploitation, no matter how politically expedient the solution may appear in the short run.

While numerous areas of honest disagreement exist, we believe our proposal does satisfy the necessary economic and financial criteria. Our proposal contains five principal components, each of which is discussed in some detail in later sections.

In the summary here, items A, B, C, and D are required to resolve the uncertainty surrounding the financial future of the system that presently exists. Beyond that, it is necessary to redesign the system so as to eliminate the defects which have led to its present financial predicament. Item E addressed the redesign problem.

A. As the benefit formulas are written in present law, increases in the cost of living ultimately are doubly reflected in the relative benefits granted to successive annual cohorts of retirees. Given the same real earnings history, inflation means that each successive group of retirees receives a higher pension in the same year as retirees of an earlier cohort group. This effect is referred to as "coupling" and should be eliminated. Retirees who had the same real lifetime gross earnings should receive the same real pensions irrespective of the year in which they reached retirement age.

B. Currently, gainful employment for the elderly between 65 and 72 years of age can lead to reduced benefits and even to a full disallowance of all benefits. This "retirement test" should be entirely eliminated. Benefits should be paid in full irrespective of the source or amount of the recipient's income.

C. Currently, all social security benefits are tax exempt and half of all social security contributions are tax exempt. The tax treatment of social security benefits should be brought in line with that of other pensions and retirement annuities. That is, half of all social security benefits should be subject to personal income tax.

D. The age at which full social security benefits commence should be raised from 65 for persons presently aged less than 55. The change in the age at which retirement benefits start should be phased in gradually to allow those affected sufficient time to adjust. For example, retirement benefits could commence at age 66 for the population currently in the 45–54 age group; 67 for the 35–44 age group; and 68 for people 34 and under. A continuous progression would clearly be in order here.

E. In the long run, the social security system should be based on the principle of "dollar in dollar out." Members of the social security system should contribute, given actuarial realities, according to their future benefits. Contributions received from identifiable groups should not be collected on the premise that they will be used to pay benefits to other groups.

THE ECONOMIC ISSUES

The primary economic issues are evidenced by the fact that the social security system has a substantial unfunded net liability. The "actuarial deficiency" was estimated officially in 1975 at $2.1 trillion and the unfunded liability at $2.7 trillion (U.S. Treasury Department, 1975). Even the lower figure is the equivalent of $10,000 per man, woman, or child alive in the United States today. Alternative economic and demographic assumptions and other accounting techniques could give much higher figures.

The unfunded liability, in conjunction with the long-standing rapid decline in U.S. birth rates, and the failure to take remedial action, portends a serious financing problem. According to some scholars, the unfunded liability also corresponds to a capital stock deficiency and thereby to restrained worker productivity. In addition to any possible capital shortage, the unfunded liability is also closely related to the degree to which job creation is being discouraged in the United States. These effects have important implications for future economic growth and living standards in America.

By one perspective, the unfunded liability of the social security system is analogous to government debt. The conventionally defined debt is merely the discounted cash value of the promise of the government to make interest payments in the future on its officially recognized liabilities. The current amount of the conventionally defined debt held by the private sector is about $400 billion. Likewise, the unfunded liability is the discounted net cash flows implicit in the Social Security Act. Although the unfunded liability is harder to estimate than conventional debt, it is no less to be regarded as a commitment under present law to future net expenditure. However, unlike the explicit public debt, its real magnitude is only indirectly related to a government decision to let the purchasing power of the dollar decline. Benefits as well as tax receipts have adjustments for inflation.

By another perspective, the unfunded liability of the system can be interpreted as the amount the government would have to pay the private insurance industry to assume responsiblity for the entire social security system. The cash flows included in such a hypothetical transfer would include the privilege to tax workers as currently legislated as well as the obligations to pay benefits.

Finally, the unfunded liability represents the amount the government would have to pay to compensate current social security participants if it were to disband the system. It is what a "hold-harmless" provision would cost if the government were to switch from the current social security system to, say, a negative income tax or some other such system (Hobbs & Powlesland, 1975).

Computationally, the unfunded liability is the net discounted cash outflow associated with all current members of the social security system. The cash flows include both expected benefits to be paid out over the years and expected receipts to be collected from employers and employees. The discount rate used approximates actual market interest rates on government debt.

There are several methods used to calculate the unfunded liability in actual practice. The official concept of the unfunded liability looks solely at the projected cash flow of the entire system (including any new members) for 75 years and discounts back to the present. This method understates the deficiency because it includes taxes paid by many workers prior to the 75 year cut-off date, but excludes benefits which do not become payable until after the cut-off date.

It is far more informative to look at the "closed group" of workers already in the system. With only current members in mind, the discounted cash flow then equals the unfunded liability. Even if the closed-group concept is used, numerous additional assumptions are required, such as inflation rates, real wage growth, mortality, and so on. In Table 6–3, we show just how sensitive these calculations can be. In Table 6–1, we have listed the "official estimates" of the closed group's unfunded liability over the last several years.

From strictly a financing standpoint, an unfunded liability would have little meaning as long as the working population is growing sufficiently rapidly. With ever-increasing numbers of young workers entering the economy, the government can pay the retired benefits by taxing the young directly at a stable rate of taxation. The financing of benefits does not in itself mandate a funded system so long as there is sufficient growth of the working population.

When the working population grows more slowly than the population of beneficiaries—that is, when population growth rates are declining—the ability of the government to finance benefits without funding depends on ever-increasing tax rates imposed on young workers. Without increasing tax rates, there would have to be a scaling down of benefits per retired worker. If, for whatever reason, there is a problem associated with raising tax rates on the incomes of young workers, then the financing capacity of the social security system is jeopardized. This is precisely one basis of current concerns. The question is whether the social security system can be considered "sound."

In the last fifteen years, we note a resumption of the rapid decline in U.S. fertility rates. Following the postwar baby boom, fertility rates have fallen well below the rate needed to sustain zero population growth. The precipitous decline is apparent in Table 6–2. As a

Table 6–1. Unfunded Liability of the OASDI 1969 to 1975—Closed-Group Concept Official Estimates *(billions of dollars)*

Year	*Unfunded Liability*
1967	$ 350
1968	414
1969	330
1970	415
1971	435
1972	1,865
1973	2,118
1974	2,460
1975	2,710

Source: U.S. Treasury Department (1975 and earlier years). The underlying assumptions vary from year to year.

Table 6–2. Fertility Rates *(expected children per woman during childbearing years)*

Year	Rate	Year	Rate
1958	3.63	1970	2.43
1960	3.61	1971	2.25
1962	3.43	1972	2.00
1964	3.17	1973	1.87
1966	2.68	1974[a]	1.82
1968	2.43	1975[a]	1.79

[a]Estimated from incomplete data.

Source: Unpublished data from the Office of the Actuary, Social Security Administration.

Table 6–3. Old Age, Survivors' and Disability Insurance (OASDI): Projected Expenditures as a Percent of Taxable Payroll under Three Alternative Sets of Economic and Demographic Assumptions

Year	1[a]	2[b]	3[c]	Tax Rate in Present Law
1975	10.9%	10.9%	10.9%	9.9%
1990	11.1	12.1	13.0	9.9
2000	11.7	13.4	15.3	9.9
2010	12.8	16.0	19.6	9.9
2020	15.5	21.3	28.2	11.9
2030	17.2	26.0	37.1	11.9
2040	16.6	27.4	42.1	11.9
2050	16.3	28.6	46.0	11.9

[a] Assumes (1) ultimate fertility rate rises to 2.3 (births per woman during lifetime); (2) inflation 3 percent *per annum*; (3) real wage growth 2.25 percent *per annum*; and (4) unemployment averaging 4.5 percent of the labor force.

[b] Assumes (1) ultimate fertility rate of 1.9; (2) inflation 4 percent; (3) real wage growth 1.75 percent; and (4) 5 percent unemployment.

[c] Assumes (1) ultimate fertility 1.7; (2) inflation 5 percent; (3) real wage growth 1.25 percent; and (4) 5.5 percent unemployment.

Source: U.S. Board of Trustees of the Federal OASDI 1976.

result of these rapid and fundamental changes in demographic trends in conjunction with individual benefit formulas, we get the following types of implied tax rates just to maintain legislated benefit payments on a pay-as-you-go basis.

A financing problem cannot arise if social security is fully funded. A retardation of birth rates would have no effect on social security tax rates or on benefit levels. Variations in population growth rates will make the trust fund contract or expand, but will not change the benefits per retiree or the taxes per worker.

According to Feldstein and others, the unfunded liability also leads to a capital shortage (see Feldstein, 1974, 1975; and Laffer and Ranson, 1973). The argument proceeds along the following lines. People with assured retirement benefits will save less of their income than they otherwise would. Because their old age is already provided for, one reason to save is eliminated. As a consequence, total savings is reduced. A portion of income, instead of going into savings and real capital formation, will be consumed. This, in due course, results in a smaller capital stock and lower output per worker.

A more general argument returns to the theme of the separation of economic effort from reward. The propensity of the economy to accumulate capital is a function, in part, of the extent to which the income from capital is taxed when generated. If tax rates on income are to be higher in the future than they are today, there is a substitution effect away from future production; that is, capital formation will be lowered.

To keep output and productivity high, the social security system would have to offset this anticapital effect. To do so completely, the social security system must be fully funded. Full funding of liabilities is one way of acquiring real assets to protect against an impending shortfall in taxes from the working population.

In addition to the savings issue, there are other factors at work which reduce economic activity and national income. In general, an additional dollar of social security taxes paid by an individual does not earn that individual a current dollar's worth of future benefits. The marginal benefits one obtains through the social security system are not directly related to the marginal taxes paid. That is, social security, as the system is presently designed, leads to a disassociation between effort and reward. The unfunded liability, in part, corresponds to this disassociation.

Over the years, participants in the social security system have paid into the system substantially less than they have received or will receive. A similar pay-as-you-go formula that facilitated this historical redistribution will have just the opposite impact on subsequent generations. Current workers' taxes are going directly as benefits to current retirees. Nothing is put aside for current workers' benefits later on when they retire. Current workers must rely entirely on obtaining their benefits through higher tax rates on future workers.

A widely recognized proposition in economics is that if a commodity is taxed, there will generally be less of it. Symmetrically, if a commodity is subsidized, generally there will be more of it. The quantity effects should be greater the longer the tax or subsidy is expected to remain in place. The social security system, as currently constituted, taxes work, output, and employment through the payroll tax. Furthermore, benefits are paid conditionally on the requirement that recipients do not work. Therefore, the current system subsidizes nonwork, leisure, and nonparticipation in the labor force. An unfunded social security system, such as the one the United States currently has, restrains work, output, and employment and stimulates nonwork, leisure, and unemployment.[1]

Firms hire an employee based, in part, upon the total cost to the firm of hiring the employee. The costs associated with the hiring of an employee may be tangible or intangible, but a rational firm will consider all of them in its hiring decision. The higher the total cost to the firm, the fewer employees the firm will hire. The demand curve for employees is downward-sloping with regard to the effective cost of employment borne by firms.

But employees, in deciding where or whether to work, do not care how much their employment costs the firm. Employees are concerned with how much money they will receive. If nothing else changes, the more employees receive the more willing they are to work. The supply of employees' services is upward-sloping with regard to the effective compensation received.

The difference between what it costs a firm to hire an employee and what the employee effectively gets paid is called the wedge. The wedge acts as a direct disincentive to employment. The disincentive effect operates simultaneously through restraining the firm's demand for employees and through restraining a potential employee's willingness to work.

If the current social security (OASDI plus HI) tax is taken by itself and a worker is paid $100 per week in gross wages, then it costs the firm $105.85 to employ the worker inclusive of the employer's part of the social security tax. Similarly, the employee does not receive the full $100. After deducting the worker's portion of the social security tax, the employee is left with $94.15.

In total, it costs the firm $105.85 a week to hire the employee, and yet the employee only receives $94.15. There is a wedge of $11.70 or 11.7 percent between what a firm must pay and what the worker receives.

It is clear what would result if the social security tax were raised from the current 5.85 percent employer and employee rates to 12.5 percent on both parties' parts. Whereas before it cost the employer $105.85 to hire an employee, it would now cost $112.50. Likewise, the employee who previously received $94.15, would now receive $87.50. This increase in social security tax rates reduces both the

1. For a review of the effects of Social Security on economic incentives, together with a discussion of the evidence, see Feldstein (1976).

firm's demand for workers and the worker's willingness to work. Output and employment are lowered.

The bias against output and employment would be fully neutralized if the expected present value of social security benefits earned by an incremental dollar of taxes were equal to one dollar. The social security system would then be viewed as no more economically undesirable than a program of fringe benefits or payment in kind. This is not the case, however, for the U.S. system. The link between the marginal contribution and the marginal benefit is not close (see Brittain, 1972).

As can be seen under present legislation (see Table 6−3), there will sooner or later have to be a sharp increase in the payroll tax. Each worker will have to pay more relative to wages in order for each retiree to receive what has been promised. If the benefit schedules in present law remain in force, payroll tax rates will have to rise to unprecedented levels. By enlarging the wedge, these higher tax rates, if tolerated politically, would materially reduce total employment. In our view it is unlikely that such high taxes will be tolerated politically.

In our view, there is absolutely no question that actual benefits received in the future will be lower than they are currently promised to be. What remains to be seen is how soon, how much, and in what manner they will be reduced. The current social security law, especially when viewed in conjunction with other federal, state, and local programs, has promised more than the society will be willing to deliver. Indeed, taking into account the direct disincentive effects on capital formation, employment, and output, there may even be more promised than society would be physically able to deliver.

Many of our political leaders and social pundits have inadvertently proselytized policies that would lead, if carried to their ultimate conclusion, to the destruction of the production base upon which all beneficence finally rests. This is both counterproductive and inhumane.

MAJOR ELEMENTS OF THE PROPOSAL

A. The social security cost-of-living escalator should be changed (decoupled). Dollar benefits should be indexed so that price rises have no effect on real benefits paid. Retirees who had the same real earnings history should receive the same real retirement benefits independent of their retirement year.

The legislated benefit formulas prescribe that a retiree receive an automatic pension increase that reflects the rise in the consumer price index. That is, a retired person receives annual benefits which remain constant in purchasing power terms. Another aspect of the formulas, which takes on an important role later, is that benefit payments have progressivity built into them. As lifetime earnings and taxes rise, social security benefits rise less than proportionately.

The formulas further govern the relative treatment of people who reach age 65 in different years. In actual practice, using the formulas, it turns out that the later the year of retirement, the more generous the benefits. Each year's cohort of retirees obtains a higher annual pension in terms of constant purchasing power units than previous years' retirees, even when real earnings histories were held the same. The higher the rate of inflation, the greater is the discrepancy. The increase in social security benefits from one year's cohort to the next includes both a full allowance for the year's inflation and a rise that fully reflects the rise in nominal wages. This feature of current legislation is known as "coupling" because, in the long run, increases in the cost of living are doubly reflected in benefit increases. The base rises in relation to nominal wages and the benefit-to-wage ratio rises through an explicit cost-of-living escalator. As a consequence, aggregate real social security outlays rise over time at a rate which is itself an increasing function of the rate of inflation. (For a more detailed exposition of the benefit formula, and the automatic adjustment for inflation, see Campbell, 1976.)

The many different ways of eliminating this feature are referred to as "decoupling." The specific formula changes are often complex. Two broad alternatives eliminate the extra cost-of-living escalator, and rely upon gains in earnings to reflect rises in the cost of living in the long run. In both cases the rate of inflation would no longer be a factor in the growth rate of real expenditures over time. The alternative supported by Social Security Administration officials would program benefits for each cohort as a whole to exceed those of the preceding cohort in full proportion to the differences in lifetime average pre-tax earnings. The second alternative, proposed by a Congressionally appointed panel of economists and actuaries led by William Hsiao of Harvard, would program real benefits to rise less than in full proportion to wages over time (Consultant Panel on Social Security, 1976). The financial difference between these proposals is significant.

Under the Hsiao proposal, two people of the same real lifetime gross earnings who reach retirement age in different years would receive the same real annual pension. Under the Social Security Administration proposal, the younger person would receive more. This higher amount reflects, under the Social Security Administration schema, (i) the fact that the younger retiree stood lower in the frequency distribution of earnings relative to his age peers; and (ii) the fact that the ratio of benefits to lifetime earnings falls with increases in lifetime earnings due to the progressive nature of the current benefit structure. The Social Security Administration proposal is designed to provide that two people who are of the same relative standing in the frequency distribution of earnings, but who reach retirement age in different years, enjoy the same ratio of benefits to lifetime earnings. Under the Hsiao proposal, the younger of two persons at the same frequency in the earnings distribution would receive a slightly lower ratio (as a result of the progressive benefit structure) of benefits to earnings because his or her real earnings would be higher.

In our view, the Hsiao proposal is preferable. In light of the financial stringencies, it is certainly the more attractive. There is no logical or moral reason from our perspective why the progressivity of the benefit structure should be retained with respect to people of different earnings but of the same age, and yet repealed with respect to people of different ages. In effect, the Social Security Administration proposal is building into the system an automatic growth in scale for which there is no visible economic or social justification.

If the entire proposal we advance here were accepted, the distinction would be rather minor in the steady state due to the "dollar-in-dollar-out" feature discussed under Section E below.

B. The retirement test should be entirely eliminated. Benefits earned should be paid in full irrespective of the recipient's earned income.

Throughout history, mankind has revered the repository of wisdom, experience, and skills possessed by the aged. In the United States today, however, this tradition has been undermined on a national scale. Built into the social security system is a major deterrent to employment of the aged: the retirement test.

At the age of 65, workers receive full security benefits only by restricting their earned income. Above the $2,760 exempt annual amount, the more they earn, the less they receive in social security benefits. This provision of our social security system is equivalent to an earned-income tax surcharge of 50 percent. In effect, people between the ages of 65 and 72 are subject to sharply higher tax rates than are other members of society.[2]

2. The president's 1976 budget recommends tightening the restrictiveness by applying the retirement test on an annual basis.

Although we are not familiar with any extensive empirical documentation, we expect that the retirement test discourages many would-be workers. Most people remain able to work at the age of 65 and beyond. A number of these would like to augment their retirement incomes. Output, income growth, and the general level of economic well-being are all reduced by the fact that this desire to work is substantially frustrated.

We can ill afford such a dissipation of a unique national resource. While our wealth may be great, gratuitous waste is intolerable. We think it is pernicious to effectively deny society access to the skills and abilities of its aged members. Moreover, it is transparently unjust to require the elderly to work under confiscatory taxes. Ironically, the provisions that reduce social security benefits of the 65 to 72 age group as their earnings rise is an onerous taxation of the very group the system's mission is to help. The retirement test is uneconomic and immoral.

It is sometimes argued that we cannot "afford" to eliminate the retirement test because it would impose a "cost" in terms of federal budget outlays.[3] Even if this were so, it is beside the point, since we should evaluate policy changes in terms of true economic costs and not budgetary inflows and outflows. In any case, in all likelihood, elimination of the retirement test would have little or no adverse effect on the budget deficit. Higher earned incomes of the 65 to 72 year olds would lead to added federal revenue, at least partly offsetting the benefit payments restored by eliminating the test. We can think of no economic reason why such a retirement test should not be discarded immediately.

C. The tax treatment of social security benefits should be brought in line with that of other pensions and retirement annuities. That is, half of all social security benefits should be liable to federal, state, and local income taxes.

In virtually all private retirement plans, either benefits are taxed or contributions are taxed. In the instance of our current social security system, the employer's portion of contributions is not liable to taxation when made. This proportion is a tax adjustable expense item to the firm. The benefits attributable to the employer's portion of contributions also are not liable to tax when received. Social security benefits are exempt from income tax. This feature of tax law is tantamount to differential tax treatment for like economic situations.

3. The net increase in budget outlays has recently been estimated at $3 billion per annum.

It discriminates against private arrangements for retirement insurance in favor of governmental arrangements.

Taxation of half of social security benefits would have the effect of lower benefit payments in the aggregate. In addition, the tax change would have a major distributive impact. Only those people who have sufficient other income will in practice pay significant additional taxes. They, of course, are presumably the ones least in need. As a consequence, making half of social security benefits subject to income tax will not increase revenues at the expense of the poor.

Making half of the benefits subject to income tax will tend to reduce outlays at present and under the current program taxation of half the benefits might reduce net outlays by as much as $3.5 billion. It will also tend to mitigate any increased outlay effect generated by elimination of the retirement test, because as the aged work and earn income, their tax brackets rise.

D. The age at which full social security benefits commence should be raised from 65 for persons less than 55. For example, it should be 66 for those people in the age group 45 to 54. People between 35 and 44 should start receiving benefits at 67, and people under 34 years of age should start receiving benefits at age 68.

While the other features of our reform proposal in aggregate would substantially help the economic and financial soundness of the social security system, this provision remains essential. The unfunded liability has to be eliminated.

It is our view that relief should flow most to those least able to adapt themselves to broken promises. Thus, if promised social security benefits are to be reduced, as we believe they must, they should be reduced most for those who can adjust and least for those who cannot adjust. People who are currently living on social security benefits should not have their benefits reduced. Being elderly, they can do little if anything to change their circumstances. People whose benefits are far away in time should bear the lion's share of any adjustment. The more distant the expected benefits, the more adjustment these people can make.

It would be far preferable never to have erred in a way to require reneging on promises. Such is, unfortunately, not the case. The society has promised more than will be forthcoming. In one way or another, these promises will be reneged upon. It is too late to ask whether this is right or wrong. The serious moral questions remaining are how much will be reneged, when, at what cost, and to whom. We believe the least harmed are those who can plan alternative retirement arrangements. Peoples' flexibility is directly related to the length of their planning horizons. Therefore, the youngest today should, to the extent necessary, bear the principal brunt of the costs of reneging.

Under our proposal, a person who will start receiving benefits at a later date will have many years to adjust. Some may just wish to continue working the extra time when they reach 65, while others may wish to save more and retire at the date they originally planned. In either case, time horizons would be sufficiently long to allow for change in commencement of benefits without undue hardship.

E. The objective of any legislated social security program should be to provide proper old age and survivors insurance to the American people. Whether mandatory or voluntary, this insurance should be properly priced on an individual basis. Each person should receive in value terms approximately what that individual pays.

The concept of principle of "dollar in dollar out" should be a clear goal for the steady state social security system. Once the issues surrounding the current unfunded liability have been resolved, groups of individuals should no longer be asked to pay more or less than they can actuarially expect to receive. For any member of the social security system, each dollar's contribution to the program should, on a one-for-one basis, be associated with a dollar's worth of expected future benefits. A one-for-one relationship between effort and reward is a required characteristic of any rational program.

In our opinion, the contribution rate should be allowed to vary, while benefit levels should become the primary objective of government policy. It appears to us that a desire to have a social security program arises out of a desire to maintain a living standard for the elderly. As such, policy should be directed at the explicit objective of the population: social security benefits. Tax rates should therefore adjust to the realities of the actuarial tables and the desired level of benefits. Tax rates should be calculated group by group on a dollar-in-dollar-out principle.

ADDITIONAL CONSIDERATIONS

Many other moral issues arise in the complex structure of the social security system as it is currently legislated. These issues range from whether like circumstances receive like treatment, income distribution, reneging of government obligations, and the appropriate treatment of women.

In several areas we see serious and important detailed reforms needed, but we do not have specific recommendations. We therefore shall only mention the problems. Benefit formulas should take into account all contributions, not merely wages during a select number of years.

Contributions should be made in order to receive benefits, not just as a tax on wages. Thus, social security contributions should be made irrespective of whether the individual works or is unemployed.

Secondary income redistributive programs should be instituted to ameliorate any hardships these modifications might cause specific individuals or groups. The concept of income should, wherever appropriate, be used in place of wages. And women should be treated on a par with men.

The most discussed moral issue vis-à-vis the social security system is its effect on overall income distribution. It is our view that the redistributive aspects of the current program are virtually impossible to disentangle. While the fact of how income is in reality redistributed is extremely important, we are unable to make even an educated guess as to whether the lower-income groups are benefited or hurt, let alone by how much. As we shall try to show here, the crosscurrents and analytic difficulties are so great as to leave the issue totally unresolved.

Irrespective of age, the social security (OASDI plus HI) tax currently applies to wages up to $15,300 per *annum.* The total contribution rate is 11.7 percent of these wages. This tax rate applies exclusively to earnings and to no other form of income. The rate does not change within the $0 to $15,300 range.

As a result of the flat tax rate with a wage ceiling, workers who earn more than $15,300 annually pay the maximum tax amount of $1,790, inclusive of the employer contribution. Therefore, as a percent of wages from $15,300 and higher, the average tax rate falls with earnings. In sum, looking at the relation of the tax to workers' earned incomes a one point in time, the tax is proportional (neither regressive nor progressive) in respect to earnings until the wage of $15,300 is reached. From that level, the tax *per se* is regressive.

Insofar as nonwage income accrues disproportionately more to the upper and lower tails of the income distribution, then the social security tax is progressive in the lower-income range, perhaps approximately neutral for middle-income groups, and regressive at higher levels.

The impact of social security on cross-sectional income distribution is far more complicated than the impact of the tax side alone. In general, we would have to include in the analysis the benefit side also, and the interaction between taxes paid and benefits received. Finally, there are better ways to look at income distribution than the pure cross-sectional perspective: for example, there is redistribution across time, redistribution across age groups, and redistribution across lifetime income.

Looking at the cross-sectional distribution of benefits, we find that recipients tend to have low wages. This is partly a matter of age, and partly a result of the retirement test. Considering the system as a pure cross-sectional transfer, there is little doubt that, in the aggregate, net benefit-recipient groups tend to have lower wages than net taxpaying groups. Of course, this in no way signifies that the system is progressive in any meaningful respect.

Looking at distribution over time, regressive aspects again appear. Higher-income people tend to join the system later in life than lower-income people, because of the extended number of years of education usually associated with higher income. Thus, there are years when higher-income people pay little and lower-income people pay more.

The benefit formulas also miss a phenomenon with important distributive implications. Higher-income people tend to live longer than lower-income people. Higher-income people therefore collect benefits from the social security system for more years than do lower-income people.

In sum, people with higher lifetime earnings pay less and receive more than the legislated tax and benefit tables would suggest at first sight. People with lower lifetime earnings tend to pay more and receive less than the tables initially suggest.

Numerous other considerations cloud and confuse the issue of income distribution. It is our view that incentive effects have had a major impact on the redistributive aspects of the social security system. The appropriate question is, What would the income distribution have been had there not been a social security system? While the issue is important, we do not know even the direction of the effect. As a general rule, we feel that income redistribution should not be a primary objective of the social security system *per se.*

As some stage it might well be worthwhile to make voluntary some aspects of social security participation. The principal impetus for having a social security program is to assure that people are provided for in their old age. It would seem reasonable that major elements of the program could be dispensed with if an individual could be exempted by making alternative provisions sufficient for old age. The only government intervention required for such an individual may be a government guarantee against bankruptcy. But voluntarization is only possible once financial soundness is attained. Voluntarism otherwise would lead to a further erosion of financial soundness. Good risks will in general opt out while bad risks will remain.

With the advent of financial and economic soundness, an entirely new set of economic and moral issues will arise. How does, and should, the government allocate the resources that accumulate from a fully funded system? The potential of a problem arising from governmental control of this magnitude of real resources is self-evident. Still, the need for a fully funded reserve remains. The magnitude of the problem can be seen by the size of the trust fund that would currently exist if the social security system had been properly funded all along. As mentioned earlier, it would amount to a minimum of $2.7 trillion! However, even if we began to fund the system now, it would be many decades before amounts of such magnitude were accumulated.

Our preference here would be to have the government accept bids on the management of portfolios as the assets accumulate. A predetermined set of explicit criteria would be used for portfolio contract renewals. The government would be allowed no voting privileges whatsoever over the trust funds' asset holdings. In both spirit and legal fact, the government should act purely as a trustee or an intermediary for the public. Guarantees against the possibility of manipulating the trust fund assets for political or other noneconomic purposes must be made.

REFERENCES

Brittain, John A. (1972). *The Payroll Tax for Social Security.* Washington: Brookings Institution.

Campbell, Colin D. (1976). *Overindexed Benefits: The Decoupling Proposals for Social Security.* Washington: American Enterprise Institute.

Consultant Panel on Social Security (1976). "Report to the United States Congressional Research Service of a panel led by William Hsiao." April.

Feldstein, Martin (1974). "Social Security, Induced Retirement, and Aggregate Capital Accumulation," *Journal of Political Economy* 82: 905–26.

—— (1975). "Toward a Reform of Social Security," *The Public Interest,* (Summer), pp. 75–95.

—— (1976). "Social Insurance." Unpublished manuscript presented at the Conference on Income Distribution, American Enterprise Institute, Washington, D.C., May 20.

Hobbs, Charles D., and Stephen L. Powlesland (1975). *Retirement Security Reform: Restructuring the Social Security System.* Concord, Vermont: Institute for Liberty and Community.

Kaplan, Robert S., and Roman L. Weil (1974). "An Actuarial Audit of the Social Security System." Report to the Secretary of the Treasury.

Laffer, Arthur B. (1975). "Comments on the Social Security System." Paper presented at the Conference on Ethics and the Aging Society, University of Chicago.

____ and R. David Ranson (1973). "Some Economic Consequences of the U.S. Social Security System," in *Proceedings* of the 66th Annual Conference of the National Tax Association/Tax Institute of America, at Toronto, pp. 211–31.

Ranson, R. David (1976). "Financing the Social Security System." Testimony before the House Ways and Means Committee, Subcommittee on Social Security, February 4.

U.S. Board of Trustees of the Federal OASDI Trust Funds (1976). *1976 Annual Report to the Congress.* June.

U.S. Department of Health, Education and Welfare (1975). *Reports of the Quadrennial Advisory Council on Social Security.* House Document #94–75. Washington: Government Printing Office, March 10.

U.S. Treasury Department (1975). *Statement of Liabilities and Other Financial Commitments of the United States Government* ["Saltonstall Report"]. Published annually by the Fiscal Service, Bureau of Government Financial Operations.

Commentary

Comment on Laffer and Ranson

Lawrence T. Smedley

I would characterize Ranson and Laffer's paper as interesting but provocative. It is an unconventional and bold approach to social security reform. It is certainly not within the mainstream of thinking about social security reform, not even if you are on the right bank of that mainstream.

The paper begins by stating two basic objectives: (1) to rid the social security system of its massive, unfunded liability; and (2) to remove the massive and pervasive antiwork basis of the current system. The authors then outline some proposals which are expected to accomplish these objectives.

The first issue raised is the so-called unfunded liability of the social security system. The paper uses the term "unfunded liability" which is an actuarial term. If something is not fully funded, it has an unfunded liability. But no actuary, at least no responsible actuary, has ever claimed that because a retirement fund has an unfunded liability it is actuarially unsound.

The claim that the system is financially unsound with an unfunded liability of \$2.7 trillion is a false analogy with private insurance which, because of its voluntary character, cannot count on income from new entrants to fund a portion of future obligations for present participants. A compulsory social insurance system is soundly financed if, on the basis of actuarial estimates, current assets plus future income are expected to be sufficient to cover all obligations. No reputable actuary, social insurance expert, business or labor organization, Social Security Advisory Council, or congressional committee has ever recommended the kind of funding recommended by

Ranson and Laffer. In short, the unfunded liability claim is a spurious issue.

The experience of Germany illustrates this point. Germany was defeated and devastated in two world wars. It suffered both runaway inflation and catastrophic depression. Yet it was able to reconstitute its social insurance system, the world's oldest, and to insure that all those who acquired rights over all that period were paid benefits when due or have had their rights credited for future benefits. No one to my knowledge at that time bothered to compute the unfunded accrued liability of the German system. That would have been absolutely meaningless.

In fairness to the authors, they did not make their case solely on the basis of unfunded liability, but also on the issue of a capital shortage and a need for greater capital formation. I am no authority on the question of whether there is a capital shortage. But it is an issue which divides economists and on which there is no clear consensus.

For example, a number of economists recently completed a study of the social security financing problem for the Senate Finance Committee and the House Ways and Means Committee. They could not agree on the importance of this supposed capital shortage. However, they were unanimous in opposing heavier funding of the system even if it did exist and stated:

> If it is felt that there is too little capital accumulation in the current economy, this is a problem which can be influenced by a large variety of fiscal and monetary policies. Especially since the payroll tax, considered as a source of capital formation, is not a progressive tax, like the income tax, it seems to us inappropriate to use the payroll tax to finance a major portion of any desired capital increase.

In short, it would be most unfair to use a regressive payroll tax to solve either an alleged or real shortage of capital and place that burden on the backs of workers.

Then the authors discuss what they feel are the antiwork biases of the U.S. social security system. I hate to discuss the retirement test again—we have already discussed it in some detail—but I would like to reemphasize the principle involved. Social security insures against loss of income due to death, disability, or retirement. If the contingency insured against does not occur, the program does not pay benefits. You do not collect your fire insurance unless you have a fire, you do not collect your accident insurance unless you have an accident, and so forth. The retirement test simply measures whether the contingency insured against, retirement, has occurred. You may differ with this principle, but I do not believe it is fair to characterize it as immoral. This characterization by the authors was too strong a term to describe it.

It is true that the retirement test applies only to earned income. By paying benefits regardless of other financial resources, social security serves as a base on which other forms of protection, such as investments, savings, insurance, and the like, can be built. Withholding benefits because of sources other than nonwork would reduce incentive for savings and would make it impossible for most people to make provisions for a more financially secure old age than would be possible by social security benefits alone. It would also jeopardize the eligibility of private pension recipients to receive social security benefits. It would also increase the danger of the introduction of a means test for social security benefits.

But only 1.4 million—about 6 percent of the 22 million people age 65 and older—have any benefits withheld under the retirement test. Its elimination would benefit primarily those 500,000 persons who are working full time and not drawing any social security benefits.

The large majority of aged persons are unable to work because of poor health or lack of employment opportunities. Obviously, this is a group for which full-time work cannot be expected to be a satisfactory means of supplementing social security benefits.

This same point can be made about their proposal for raising the age of eligibility for social security benefits. Such a proposal may save the program some money, but in the absence of full employment the most likely result would be more elderly on SSI and welfare with little or no economic gain to society, with less dignity and satisfaction to the individual and with a resulting decline in social harmony. In any event, the potential for active workers among the elderly are not great even under the best of economic conditions. Data from the Social Security Administration's Retirement History Project showed that more than 70 percent of workers retired early either because of poor health (54 percent) or for other involuntary reasons (17 percent). Extremely few of the latter were due to compulsory retirement; the overwhelming majority were due to layoffs or discontinued jobs.

The retirement test provides that social security benefits are payable in full if a person's annual earnings remain below $2,760. If earnings exceed that amount, the social security benefit is reduced one dollar for two dollars of earnings in excess of $2,760. Many economists oppose the retirement test on the grounds it has an adverse, significant impact on labor-force participation by older people. However, many of the same economists support negative income tax and guaranteed income proposals which have formulas providing lower exempt amounts of income and tax offsets equal to or far less liberal than that allowed by the retirement test. It makes one wonder whether these economists may be more interested in discrediting the social security program rather than making an objective evaluation of its provisions.

The authors also discuss and have policy suggestions for the so-called "decoupling" problem—a very complicated issue. The 1975 law automatically adjusts the law's benefit table for future retirees whenever present retiree benefits are automatically increased to reflect the rise in living costs. In addition, workers' earnings normally increase during their working lives and these higher earnings increase the average wage on which their benefits are based. Thus, the future benefit formula reflects periodic cost-of-living adjustments of the benefit table plus increases in the worker's wage. Thus, the future replacement ratios—the percentage of wages paid in benefits at time of retirement—will vary depending on the relative movement of prices and wages and could be more or less than the current ratios.

Under present actuarial assumptions, this combination is more than enough to keep up with prices and wages, and in the next century, benefits could exceed the highest earnings of some beneficiaries. Congress clearly would not let this happen. "Decoupling" would cut this cost at least in half. However, since the social security trustees have made their actuarial projections on the assumption Congress will not act, their estimates create the impression that the trust funds face an unmanageable long-range financial problem. Similarly, Ranson and Laffer in their paper never explain or put into perspective these cost factors and simply put forth horrendous cost calculations which are misleading since they will never occur.

There are a number of ways to "decouple." The approach which has wide consensus support—ranging from the Ford Administration to the AFL–CIO—would stabilize the present wage replacement ratios for the working population on into the future. This is called indexing by average wages. The authors, on the other hand, would index by prices so that ratios in the future would decline. In other words, the percentage of benefits relative to wages at time of retirement would decrease. I hope the authors would have the courage of their convictions and would advocate a similar formula for the faculty pension at the University of Chicago. Actually, under the new pension reform legislation recently passed by Congress, such discrimination against younger workers in a private pension plan would be illegal.

Ranson and Laffer are correct that the low fertility rate, if it were to continue at levels estimated by the recent trustee's report, could have a serious impact on the financing of the social security program. This would occur because the proportion of workers supporting beneficiaries will likely be much less in the next century. In other words, a higher proportion of the nation's production by active workers will have to go to support older people—assuming the two groups maintain the same relative living standards that now exist.

The authors fail to perceive or point out that the increased portion of the nation's production that will go to the retired population will be offset by a decline in the number of younger people being supported by the economy. There will be less expenditures for supporting children, for schools, for day care, and so on, and society can shift these economic savings to supporting the large older population. In short, in any society the population at work has to support those that can not work. Looking at the total economy, the economic burden for active workers will not really change much. There will be a reduction in the need to support younger people roughly balanced by an increased need to support older people.

The financial gains that accrue to society as a whole by these compensating factors are little reflected in monetary gains to the social security program itself. Thus, the financial problem is not one faced by the nation or economy as a whole, but arises from the circumscribed manner in which the social security system is financed. The system is based on a payroll tax on active workers and on employers. Exclusive reliance on this tax, if the ratio of retired people to those at work increases significantly, will require major increases in the tax to support them. The authors give the impression this is the only alternative.

The problem is how to route some of these financial gains to society from a declining birthrate to the social security program to help pay for the higher costs required to support the elderly. Considered solely as a tax, the social security contributions are highly regressive on wage earners. It would be unfair to place the entire increased burden of supporting the elderly on wage earners and income. The best way to achieve greater tax equity and to translate financial gains elsewhere in the economy to increased revenue to the program is by general revenue contributions to the trust funds.

Ranson and Laffer conclude with a so-called "dollar-in-dollar-out proposal," once the program is fully funded as they suggest, then "each dollar's contribution to the program should, on a one-for-one basis, be associated with a dollar's worth of expected future benefits."

Their proposal lacks many specific details and is in very general terms, but from what I can determine I do not think it would work. This approach might guarantee all contributors that they would get back everything contributed plus interest. However, it appears to me the proposal has a number of serious defects. Low-income workers would lose the favorable treatment now provided by the social security program's weighted benefits. Though the tax is regressive, it is balanced by progressive benefits. If low-income workers wished to participate, the proposal would tax them unfairly. In addition, the proposal has no way to adjust benefits for inflation which would injure middle-income wage earners as well as those less well off. It is also on a voluntary basis, so there would be adverse selection. The low-income workers could not participate, and the high-income workers would not. Thus, the likely end result would be that society would still have to devise some supplemental program to help take care of those who suffer loss of income due to death, disability, or retirement, and society would have to pay for it. Their basic social security program with its declining wage replacement ratios would not be adequate.

One concluding observation which is based on the impression I received by reading the conference papers and by listening to the comments made today. A social program should not be looked at or evaluated solely from an economic viewpoint. The social security system in this country is popular because it conforms to and has developed out of the cultural, psychological, and sociological factors of our society. It is not simply an economic institution. Congress in modifying and improving the social security program basically has done what the public has wanted. In short, Congress has responded to public pressures. This is what democracy is all about.

Too many economists derive their theories and models in a vacuum and expect society to change and adjust to conform to them. It is the economists who should make the adjustments and bring their thinking into greater conformity with the real world.

Chapter 7

The Future Role of Social Security

John L. Palmer

A number of developments have resulted in a growing debate over reforms of the social security system. Among these are: the recession and the resulting current financial deficits of the system; anticipated major shifts in the age distribution of the population; the automatic adjustments to the benefit formula which now result in an overadjustment to inflation for current workers and an otherwise irrational future benefit structure; the increasing labor-force participation of women and the decreasing labor-force participation of the aged; the advent of the SSI program; and the growing coverage of other public and private pensions.

The implications for social security of many of these developments have been recognized and analyzed for some years; others have gained attention only relatively recently. This paper contains a general discussion of some of the more important issues raised by these developments and the policy alternatives available for dealing with them. It suggests that in the upcoming decade and beyond several major changes in both the financing and benefit structure of social security should be considered. The most important reasons for such changes are growing inequities within the program and the potential feasibility and desirability of social security playing a more limited future role in the overall income-support picture for retired and severely disabled workers and their families.

The views expressed in this paper are the author's and should not be attributed to either the staff, officers or trustees of the Brookings Institution. This paper is adapted from a section on social security in "Income Security Policy" by John L. Palmer and Joseph J. Minarik, appearing in Henry Owen and Charles Schultze, ed., *Setting National Priorities: The Decade Ahead* (Brookings, 1976).

FINANCING

The social security system is financed on a pay-as-you-go basis. OASDI (Old-Age, Survivors and Disability Insurance) benefits are paid out of trust funds which are replenished by the payroll taxes of currently employed workers, assessed at 9.9 percent of all covered wages up to the maximum taxable individual earnings base.[1] In order to insure that current beneficiaries' payments keep pace with inflation, and in an attempt to prevent the need for continued ad hoc adjustments in the revenue structure, Congress incorporated into the social security system a set of automatic adjustments which went into effect in 1974. As a result, the maximum earnings base moves up annually at the rate of the prior year's increase in covered wages. The expectation was that under normal economic conditions this would maintain a revenue flow in close approximation to the benefit expenditure requirements on a year-to-year basis. However, largely because of the recession, OASDI is currently running annual deficits.[2] Also, projections under current law indicate long-run revenue shortfalls that increase in severity after the turn of the century. It is useful to subdivide these deficits into two—the short term (the next ten years), and the long term (the sixty-five years beyond that)—because both their basic causes and magnitude differ over these time periods, as well as the types and urgency of any policy actions that might be taken to deal with them.

In calendar year 1976, OASDI expenditures will exceed revenues by $4.4 billion, which is nearly 0.6 percent of earnings subject to the social security tax. The shortfalls will probably equal about 0.9 percent of payroll in 1981, and could go as high 1.5 percent by 1985. Reserves in the combined OASDI trust funds have not yet been depleted by the current shortfalls, but are expected to be within six years (*Social Security Trustees Report*, 1976). Deficits of this magnitude were not foreseen when, at the end of 1973, Congress last adjusted the OASDI tax schedule. This short-run deficit is due pri-

1. This base is $15,300 for calendar year 1976 and is expected to go to $16,500 for 1977. Both of these figures represent about 85 percent of the total wages of those covered by social security. In addition to this 9.9 percent payroll tax for OASDI, an additional 1.8 percent is levied on the same wage base to finance Medicare. Half of the payroll taxes are paid by the employer and half by the employee. (The self-employed pay three-fourths of this total.) There is general agreement among economists that most, if not all, of the employer's share of the tax is passed on to the employee in the form of lower wages. See Brittain (1972), Chapter III.

2. Annual deficits can be absorbed for a time by drawing down reserves in the trust funds, which were instituted to meet just such a contingency. This is presently occurring.

marily to the recent increase in unemployment and fall in real wages, both of which have reduced payroll tax receipts considerably below what was projected earlier, and also have induced a larger number of retirees. In addition, the incidence of disability among insured workers, contrary to earlier predictions, has been rising at a rapid rate. This also has contributed to the deficit.

The continuation of this short-term deficit can be predicted with a fairly high degree of certainty. (Even if the economy experiences a rapid and sustained recovery, real wage rates will be well below the level in 1980 that was originally projected in 1973.) It is not particularly sensitive to either the inflation overadjustment or likely demographic changes. Furthermore, it is unlikely that a reduction in future benefit commitments (relative to current law) would be considered as a method of dealing with it. For these reasons it can be reasonably assumed that an increase in revenues to finance social security on the order of 1.3 percent of payroll or 13 percent annually over what current law provides will be necessary over the next ten years, with at least half of it occurring within the next five years.[3]

There are three alternative sources for the additional required revenues—increases in the payroll tax rate, increases in the maximum taxable earnings base (above the level called for by the automatic adjustment), or the injection of general revenue financing into the trust funds (or some combination of two or more of these three). Whereas until recent years there has not been a great deal of resistance to either tax-rate or wage-base increases, arguments in opposition to them are gaining force because of the effects of their current high levels. Concern about the payroll tax rate centers on its overall regressive impact on the income distribution, particularly the sizable burden it represents for low-income workers and their families. Any increase in the tax rate would further exacerbate this.[4]

Increasing the wage base in order to finance the deficit would have

3. The increase is needed not only to compensate for the continuing deficit, but also to rebuild the reserves in the trust funds so that any subsequent cyclical downturns will not immediately deplete them. If one were to adopt the view that temporary injections of general revenues rather than payroll taxes should be used to finance deficits caused by cyclical fluctuations in the economy, then a permanent payroll tax increase more on the order of 8 percent, along with a transfer of general revenues in the tens of billions, might be sufficient.

4. In fact, general-revenue-financed payroll tax relief for the entire working poor population should be a high priority on the public agenda. The current temporary earned income tax credit provides "back door" payroll tax relief for low-income families with children. Expanding it to all workers on a permanent basis is one option. A more direct and comprehensive approach would be to provide family-size-related exemptions (as in the personal income tax system) that are phased out at higher income levels. See Okner (1975).

two important characteristics. First, because only a small percentage of total earnings are above the covered maximum, the limit on covered earnings would have to be raised considerably to yield the required revenues.[5] This places the entire burden on those with earnings above the current maximum and, consequently, imposes a large increase in their yearly payroll taxes. Second, these greater contributions for high-wage workers would cause them to receive higher future benefits, which may be undesirable in their own right (for reasons to be discussed below) and also would exacerbate the long-term deficit problem in the process of dealing with the short-term one.

The third alternative of utilizing some general revenue financing for social security has long been advocated by those concerned with the distributional impact of the current tax, and opposed by those concerned about perceived deterioration of the "earned-right" concept, which it is feared could lead to either or both of less political support and a means test for the system. These fears appear to be largely ungrounded, at least with respect to modest injections of general revenue financing. One approach to this was recommended by the last Advisory Council on Social Security, a public nonpartisan body appointed under statute by the President. They suggested providing general revenue financing for Medicare and gradually shifting the Medicare tax and trust funds into OASDI. This would represent no erosion of the earned-right concept because, once eligibility is established, Medicare benefits are unrelated to earnings histories.

While the short-term deficit described above can be predicted with considerable certainty, the nature of the long-term deficit depends critically upon the way in which the inflation overadjustment is eliminated (and a number of other somewhat speculative long-run economic and demographic projections). In order to understand the issues involved, it is useful to focus first upon the behavior of wage replacement rates over time. These are the ratio of a worker's initial benefit to his or her wage just prior to retirement. For workers with well-behaved earnings histories, they provided an indication of the extent to which their social security benefits alone will enable the families to maintain their prior standards of living.

5. For example, if a 0.6 percent payroll increase were to be financed this way, the wage base would have to move to approximately $22,000 in 1977. And, if the entire 1.3 percent of payroll increase were to be accomplished this way in 1977, the maximum would have to go to over $40,000. (The higher up the wage distribution one moves the fewer the workers from which to draw additional revenues.)

FUTURE BEHAVIOR OF WAGE REPLACEMENT RATES

OASDI benefits are based upon a worker's covered wage history. The first step in the computation involves determining the average monthly earnings (AME) on which payroll taxes have been paid.[6] The primary insurance amount (PIA) is then derived from the AME by applying a benefit conversion formula that in 1976 provides for 129.5 percent of the first $110 of AME, 47.1 percent of the net $290, and so on down to 20 percent of AME above $1,000. Actual monthly benefits are a fixed percentage of a worker's PIA, with the amount depending upon the characteristics of the beneficiary unit in the manner displayed in Table 7–1. This conversion formula yields a progressive replacement wage schedule, since a worker's PIA rises less than proportionately with earnings. This progressive formula was instituted on the rationale, borne out by empirical evidence, that the lower the average wage of the primary earner of a family, the more dependent the family is likely to be upon his or her social security benefits.

Under current law the future pattern of replacement rates for successive cohorts of retirees[7] can be very erratic, since the rates are influenced by three independent factors. First there is an automatic inflation adjustment which, unfortunately, was written into the 1973 law in a way that results in an overcompensation for inflation for current workers.[8] Under this provision inflation drives up replacement rates, and the greater the inflation the faster will future replacement rates rise. Concomitantly two forces are operating to depress replacement rates over time. The most important one stems from the

6. In the retirement (OA) program, for persons reaching age 62 in 1976 this is based upon the highest twenty of the past twenty-five years of earnings and is scheduled to increase to the highest thirty-five of forty by 1991. The survivors' and disability benefits have a slightly different formula for the AME calculation, but are otherwise determined similarly to OA benefits.

7. A cohort is all those retirees who enter benefit status in the same year.

8. The adjustment operates by increasing all the conversion rates in the PIA formula uniformly by the previous year's cost of living increase. Thus, if inflation in 1976 is 10 percent, the conversion rate for the first bracket in 1977 will become 142.45 percent (129.5 plus 12.95) and so on, with the final 20 percent bracket becoming 22 percent. (A new 20 percent bracket is added annually at the time the maximum wage base is automatically increased.) For current beneficiaries, whose AME does not change, this results in the desired 10 percent higher PIA and monthly benefit. Current workers are overcompensated, however, because not only do they benefit from the higher conversion rates they will face at retirement but their AMEs also will be higher because the inflation pushes up their wages over time.

Table 7–1. OASI Benefits and Replacement Rates in Second Half of 1976

	Benefit for Worker with Median Earnings	*Benefit as a Percent of PIA*[b]	*Replacement Rates*[a]		
			Worker with Low Earnings[c]	*Worker with Median Earnings*[d]	*Worker with Maximum Earnings*[e]
Worker retiring at					
Age 65	$320.00	100.0%	0.563	0.433	0.312
Age 62	252.30	80.0	0.450	0.341	0.244
Worker retiring at age 65 with spouse					
Aged 65	480.00	150.0	0.845	0.650	0.468
Aged 62	440.00	137.5	0.744	0.595	0.429
Worker retiring at age 62 with spouse					
Aged 65	410.00	130.0	0.731	0.554	0.397
Aged 62	370.60	117.5	0.661	0.501	0.358
Surviving spouse aged 65 with deceased spouse retiring in 1976 at					
Age 65	320.00	100.0	0.563	0.433	0.312
Age 62	260.20	82.5	0.464	0.352	0.252
Surviving spouse aged 62 with deceased spouse retiring in 1976 at					
Age 65	265.30	82.9	0.467	0.359	0.259
Age 62	260.20	82.5	0.464	0.352	0.252

Surviving spouse age 60 with deceased spouse retiring in 1976 at Age 65	228.80	71.5	0.403	0.310	0.223

[a] The replacement rate is the constant dollar value of the 1976 benefit divided by the constant dollar value of the 1975 wage.

[b] The PIA is the insured worker's Primary Insurance Amount. The entitlement of a single worker retiring at age 65 is equal to his PIA. All other benefits are calculated as percentages of the PIA.

[c] Worker earning half of the median wage for males over a continuous work history.

[d] Worker earning the median for all male wage and salary workers with earnings subject to the social security tax over a continuous work history.

[e] Worker earning at or above the maximum wage subject to the OASDI payroll tax over a continuous work history.

Source: U.S. Department of Health, Education, and Welfare, Office of the Assistant Secretary for Planning and Evaluation.

combination of the constant dollar bracket widths and the progressivity of the PIA conversion formula. The growth of money wages concentrates more and more of the typical worker's AME in lower PIA conversion rate brackets. This lowers the average conversion rate and, thus, replacement rates over time.[9]

The net effect on replacement rates of these three forces depends upon the assumptions made about future rates of inflation and growth of wages. Cases 1–3 of Table 7–2 illustrate, for a number of such sets of assumptions, the results for median wage workers as well as the future revenue requirements implicit for each. Examination of these cases leads to two important points. First, various feasible combinations of rates of wage and price increases can lead to extremely different behavior of replacement rates over time (even if they yield the same rate of growth of real wages as in Cases 1 and 2). It would be unsound policy to permit the vagaries of the economy to have such an arbitrary and unpredictable effect on future retirees' replacement rates.

Second, the consequence for both future benefit levels and revenue requirements of the most likely future behavior of wages and prices (something approximating Case 1) are undesirable. Replacement rates of about 65 percent are probably adequate for a median wage earner to provide for the maintenance of the standard of living achieved just prior to retirement.[10] Under Case 1 assumptions, social security replacement rates for the median wage earner will be at 50 percent and 75 percent, respectively, for individuals and couples by the turn of the century. A large portion of such workers also will be receiving private pension benefits at replacement rates of 20 percent or so, or will otherwise have the opportunity to accumulate private savings.[11] The total level of adequacy implied is likely to exceed

9. The other depressing factor is only temporary and results from the lengthening of the averaging period for the AME calculation which requires the inclusion of an additional, and typically, lower-than-average year's earnings in the AME's of each successive cohort of retirees. See Thompson (1974).

10. See Schulz et al. (1974), p. 40. The figure is arrived at by adjusting the baseline rate of 100 percent for the reduced income tax burden of the elderly (OASDI benefits are nontaxable), the discontinuation of the need to save for retirement and the lower relative expenditure needs of the elderly in order to maintain an equivalent standard of living. Similar calculations made by the Office of Income Security Policy of HEW indicate that, while 60–65 percent is appropriate for high-wage workers, the equivalent figures for median- and low-wage earners may be nearer to 70 and 80 percent, respectively.

11. Henle (June, 1972) reports that in 1972, mature private pension plans yielded a replacement rate of 15–20 percent to a worker with 20 years of service. We return below to the subject of the changing role of social security in light of growing private savings provision.

Table 7–2. OASI Replacement Rates, Revenue Requirements, and Benefit Levels under Various Economic Assumptions for Selected Years, 1980–2055

	Current Law						*Altered Law*[a]					
	Case 1: Real wage growth = 2 percent, inflation = 4 percent		*Case 2: Real wage growth = 2 percent, inflation = 6 percent*		*Case 3: Real wage growth = 1.5 percent, inflation = 4 percent*		*Case 4*[b]*: Real wage 2 percent, constant replacement rate*			*Case 5*[c]*: Real wage 2 percent, declining replacement rate*		
Year	*Re-placement rate*	*Tax rate*	*Re-placement rate*	*Tax rate*	*Re-placement rate*	*Tax rate*	*Re-placement rate*	*Benefit level (1976 dollars)*	*Tax rate*	*Re-placement rate*	*Benefit level (1976 dollars)*	*Tax rate*
1980	0.446		0.446		0.446		0.446	374.25		0.446	374.25	
1985	0.472	10.9	0.469	10.9	0.481	11.5	0.446	413.21	10.9	0.425	397.64	11.0
1990	0.471	11.1	0.476	11.1	0.489	11.8	0.446	456.22	11.1	0.403	416.50	10.2
1995	0.474	11.5	0.492	11.7	0.501	12.5	0.446	503.69	11.4	0.383	436.36	9.8
2005	0.509	12.5	0.561	13.4	0.558	14.1	0.446	614.00	11.9	0.345	479.96	9.2
2015	0.537	15.7	0.624	17.8	0.605	18.2	0.446	748.46	13.8	0.315	533.10	9.8
2025	0.558	19.9	0.677	23.8	0.643	23.7	0.446	912.37	16.6	0.290	597.88	10.9
2035	0.575	21.6	0.721	16.7	0.676	26.3	0.446	1,112.17	17.2	0.269	676.84	10.5
2045	0.589	21.5	0.756	27.4	0.705	26.7	0.446	1,355.72	16.4	0.252	773.10	9.5
2055	0.594	22.2	0.772	28.7	0.718	27.8	0.446	1,496.84	16.3	0.245	828.86	9.4

[a] Assumed to go into effect in 1980 with AMW computed over constant period of 20 years and wage-indexed.

[b] Brackets in PIA formula indexed by wage increase.

[c] Brackets in PIA formula indexed by price index.

Source: Office of the Assistant Secretary for Planning and Evaluation, HEW. These estimates may not conform precisely to comparable ones produced by the Social Security Administration, but the long-run patterns of all the variables would be quite similar.

Tax rate is the percent of payroll required to cover the current year's benefit outlays on a current cost financing basis.
All replacement rates are the PIA measured against the last year's wage in constant dollars.
PIA is for man retiring at age 65 who earned the median covered all years.
Assumptions concerning labor-force participation and other demographics are consistent with *1975 Trustee's Report*.

what society would consider desirable, especially in light of the increasingly higher rate of payroll taxation that would be required.[12]

For both these reasons there is a developing concensus among analysts and policy-makers knowledgeable about social security that steps ought to be taken as soon as possible to eliminate the inflation overadjustment and otherwise reduce the uncertainty and potential for instability in the future behavior of replacement rates. This requires an explicit policy decision about their desired future pattern. The fact that the dramatic rise in financing requirements does not come until after the turn of the century is no reason for postponing decisions. Today's benefit formula determines future financing costs. If action is postponed for too long, achieving reasonable replacement rates will require actual cutbacks in benefit levels.

Two alternatives to deal with this issue have gained the most attention. The first would hold the average replacement rate constant at, say, the 1980 level.[13] This does not imply that the real benefit levels of each successive cohort of retirees remain constant; in fact they would increase at the same rate of growth as real wage levels.[14] The future benefit levels that this would yield for median wage earners retiring in various future years and the revenue requirements (which, as a percent of covered wages, are independent of the rate of real wage growth) are displayed in Case 4 of Table 7–2. Note that even if such a measure were adopted, current projections show considerably higher long-term revenue requirements than those necessary to cover the short-term deficit. The annual amount is relatively small for the remainder of this century, but rises rapidly beyond then. This projected need is created primarily by the dramatic shift in the age distribution of the population now taking place and begins to have a major impact on social security financing as the post–World War II baby boom hits retirement age.[15]

12. Also the corresponding social security replacement rates for low-wage workers will be about 50 percent higher than for median workers. OASDI benefit levels that approach or exceed 100 percent, and thus provide for a substantially higher standard of living after retirement than just prior to it, seem to make little sense.

13. The average replacement rate can be held constant by fixing the averaging period for the AME, indexing the bracket widths in the PIA conversion formula by the growth rate of covered money wages, and applying a wage or price index to workers' past earnings in order to put all years' wages on a comparable basis when calculating AMEs. Such an approach was recommended by the last Social Security Advisory Council.

14. Historically, average annual money wage increases have exceeded inflation by about 2 percent.

15. Unless birth rates increase well above zero population growth levels in the next decade, whereas there are now approximately three workers for every aged person, there will be only two by 2020. Thus, a much larger percentage of

The second alternative would remove the inflation overadjustment in such a way that average replacement rates would decline over time with the growth of real wage levels. One future pattern of replacement rates and benefit levels for median wage earners that this could yield is displayed in Case 5 of Table 7−2.[16] Even in this instance, with average replacement rates declining fairly rapidly over time, benefit levels still increase in constant dollar terms. Revenue requirements vary from year to year, but the percentage of payroll required is considerably less than under a regime of constant replacement rates and even somewhat below current levels for most years. Patterns of reasonably behaved replacement rates intermediate to this and constant ones could be structured in line with whatever rate of increase in benefit levels relative to real wage growth, and accompanying revenue requirements, is desired.

INDIVIDUAL EQUITY[17]

When social security was set up in 1935, the relationship of an individual's benefits to payroll taxes paid was structured to more nearly resemble private insurance plans than does the present system. The goal of individual equity—that each worker should receive an amount of benefits reflecting a fair rate of return on his "contributions"—was stressed and felt to be crucial to the public acceptance of a compulsory program. Starting with the 1939 amendments, however, greater emphasis was put upon the goal of social adequacy as reflected in the minimum and dependent's benefits, the high degree of overall progressivity in the PIA computational formula and a shorter-than-lifetime contributions base for determining the AME.[18] This strong emphasis on social adequacy has been an essential element in

current wages will have to be devoted to support the same level of benefits than if this age shift did not take place. Other specific assumptions, such as those concerning labor-force participation rates and disability incidence, underlie these projections. Because of the large number of variables which must be predicted and could shift over time, projections beyond the turn of the century have a high degree of uncertainty attached to them.

16. This alternative has been advanced by the Consultant Panel on Social Security to the Congressional Research Service. It can be accomplished by taking the same steps described in footnote 14, except indexing the bracket widths in the PIA formula by the rate of increase of prices rather than money wages. Then, over time, real wage growth will result in more of the typical worker's AMW being concentrated in lower PIA conversion brackets.

17. The next three sections of this paper have benefited from drafts of a work in progress on the future of social security by Alicia H. Munnell.

18. See Pechman, Aaron, and Taussig (1968). Emphasizing social adequacy means ensuring that benefits meet some socially determined level of adequacy even though the individual equity criterion would call for less. The difference between these two is often referred to as the welfare component of social security.

social security's ability to offer a high degree of income protection relative to need, and a major source of its popularity. But, as a result of both the expanded coverage and higher benefit levels of social security and other changes that are taking place in society, the goal of social adequacy is more and more coming into conflict with that of individual equity—with increasingly controversial consequences.

The pursuit of social adequacy implies that some workers are going to receive more in benefits, relative to the taxes they pay, than others. The progressive benefit formula ensures that this will be the case for low-wage earners vis-à-vis high-wage earners. And the fact that individual earnings provide the basis for taxation while benefits are tailored to family circumstances ensures this for single workers and two-worker families vis-à-vis single-worker families. For example, a husband and wife who both work enough to be eligible for the maximum social security coverage receive only a one-third higher benefit than a couple in which the man is eligible for the maximum but the wife has no covered earnings; yet the former will have paid twice as much in taxes.

How inequitable this social adequacy emphasis appears depends largely upon the extent to which it leads to large numbers of workers in the system not realizing a fair return on their contributions. This is clearly not a problem for either current or near-term future beneficiaries. Calculations indicate that, even for a single worker at the maximum covered earnings and now at mid-career, the ratio of expected benefits to contributions, with a 2 percent real rate of return assumed on the latter, is above 1.2. No one else fares worse under the system, and this ratio ranges above 4.0 for low-wage workers with a dependent. Thus the social adequacy goal has been pursued to date without having to compromise this particular definition of individual equity at all.[19]

These very sanguine relationships between expected benefits and contributions have been made possible by a continuing rate of growth of covered workers that has far exceeded that of covered retirees in conjunction with the pay-as-you-go nature of social security financing.[20] This will no longer be the case in the future, however, because

19. A 2 percent real rate of return would be considered fair by most. This is somewhat higher than savings accounts yielded on average over the past sixty years. These calculations are reported in "Ratios of Benefits to Contributions for Selected Retirement Cases," Social Security Administration (1974). The method by which the short-term deficit is financed and the inflation overadjustment eliminated could lower these ratios, but thus are unlikely to fundamentally change this conclusion.

20. In addition to rapid growth of the labor force over the past thirty years, OASDI has increased its coverage of the private labor force from 65 to 97 percent. Most state and local government employees also have elected coverage over this same time period.

of the current broad coverage of the labor force and the shifting age distribution of the population. Young workers today and future new entrants into the labor force will find themselves facing a very different situation. Under the present method of financing, social security can only retain its social adequacy or welfare component at the very considerable expense of individual equity.[21] If social security is going to continue to be generally perceived as a fair program and to well serve those it covers, it is going to have to embody a judicious balancing of these two conflicting objectives. This suggests that a move toward more emphasis on individual equity may be required.[22] This can be pursued either on the revenue side by the use of general revenue financing to underwrite some or all of the social adequacy component of social security (and allow reduced taxation of those with otherwise inequitable rates of return), or on the benefit side by moving toward a more proportional replacement rate profile within a given age cohort across workers with different earnings histories and different family situations.

THE CHANGING ROLE OF SOCIAL SECURITY

A forceful argument in opposition to moving toward a more proportional benefit formula is that it would result in a reduced adequacy of social security benefits for those who could least afford it

21. This can be illustrated in the following way. Consider the situation in which both replacement rates and the ratio of covered workers to retirees are constant over time and payroll taxes are set at the level necessary to finance the benefit levels on a pay-as-you-go basis. In this case, the expected rate of return in the aggregate for each successive cohort of retirees is equal to the average annual rate of growth of real wages over their earnings history, which we can reasonably assume to be 2 percent. Thus, each cohort as a whole will receive a fair return on their contributions, having an average benefit-to-contributions ratio as calculated earlier of 1.0; however, to the extent any retirees in a given cohort realize a ratio greater than 1.0, others must be getting less than this 2 percent real rate of return. The only way in which every worker could realize a rate of return equivalent to the long-term rate of growth of real wages is if replacement rates were the same across all wage histories and computed on an individual rather than family basis.

In fact, the prospects for today's young workers are far worse than this hypothetical example indicates, because the ratio of covered workers to retirees will be moving in an adverse direction for them so that, under current financing arrangements, future cohorts as a whole will receive a rate of return substantially less than the rate of growth of real wages.

22. Recently, sizable numbers of state and local public employees either have withdrawn or begun to consider withdrawing from social security, partly because they can realize a higher rate of return in private or other public programs. This may well be a harbinger of decreasing support of social security by the higher-income, more steadily employed groups, who can collectively do better in alternative plans.

(that is, low-wage workers and retirees with dependents). There are, however, major changes occurring in the total income-support picture for the social security population which suggest that the future role for social security could be more limited than its present one without sacrificing on the overall adequacy of income support for the aged. In concert with other modifications to social security, these would allow for a gradual shift to a more proportional benefit formula.

The first change is the advent of the Supplemental Security Income program (SSI), the new federal guaranteed income program for the aged and disabled. This program has a highly overlapping target population with social security (approximately 50 percent of SSI recipients also receive OASDI) and is often advocated as a more appropriate vehicle than OASDI for meeting social adequacy goals for the low-income aged and disabled. In this view SSI represents a more efficient use of public funds because its income conditioning insures that benefits go only to those with a demonstrable need and its coverage of the aged and disabled poor is comprehensive. The high degree of progressivity at the lower end of the OASDI benefit formula helps many of the same poor, but does not reach others at all. It also augments the income of many elderly persons who are relatively well off because of property income or a second pension.[23] At a minimum this argues that, if society wishes to allocate efficiently additional resources to the aged and disabled population, higher priority ought to be placed upon increasing SSI rather than OASDI benefits. More strongly, it provides a rationale for reducing the degree of progressivity at the bottom end of the OASDI benefit formula in favor of higher SSI benefits.[24]

The second major change is the increased eligibility of women for OASDI and other pensions in their own right. This is a direct result of the dramatically rising labor-force participation rates of women, still on the increase, since World War II. Married couples in which both the husband and wife work now constitute a majority of families. By 1970, 68 percent of women 45–49 years of age were insured for their own social security benefits, and conservative estimates indi-

23. Retired federal civil servants are the most often cited example of this latter, but by no means predominate.

24. If this approach were pursued there are some structural changes that should be made in SSI in order to make it more substitutable for OASDI among the low-income aged and disabled. Most important would be to lower the eligibility age to 62 and to provide higher benefits for recipients with dependents not eligible for SSI in their own right. Also see Lawrence Thompson's comments in this volume for discussion of some of the issues involved in better integration of OASDI and SSI.

cate that by the turn of the century 70 percent of all wives of retired worker beneficiaries will be entitled to benefits on the basis of their own earnings record (*Report of the Quadrennial Advisory Council* 1975, p. 76). The implication of this is that the secondary spouse's benefit is rapidly becoming less necessary in order to insure adequate wage replacement for husband-wife families. Proposals to reduce or eliminate it over time should be given serious consideration.[25] If this were done, however, it would be necessary to make some provision for coverage of the minority of wives who otherwise would not qualify for social security because their work is primarily in the home. (One method for accomplishing this would be to credit half of the sum of a husband's and wife's earnings to each.)

The final major change in the broader environment of income support for the aged is the ability of higher-wage workers to save for retirement. Private pension coverage has been growing rapidly. Between 1950 and 1970 coverage more than doubled under employer financed plans from 22.5 percent of the private labor force to 48.3 percent, and the rate of asset accumulation increased about sevenfold (U.S. Department of Labor, 1974). Under the recently enacted Employee Retirement Income Security Act of 1974, standards were set up to promote greater security of private pension rights, the tax treatment of self-employed accounts was liberalized, and a new tax deduction was provided for workers without coverage from employers.

Although this trend of rapidly expanding private pension coverage appears to be arresting, the experience of the recent past indicates that increasingly middle- as well as high-wage workers will be able to supplement their social security benefits through private savings.[26] This eventually should place an upper limit on the level of compulsory public protection through OASDI. For this reason (in addition to the equity argument advanced earlier) in the future it may be desirable to reduce somewhat the degree of progressivity in the middle range of the benefit formula as real income growth occurs, as well as to slow down the rate of growth of the maximum covered earnings base. Public benefits for middle- and high-income workers as large (in real terms) as would be generated by the current automatic adjust-

25. Independent of the implications of increased labor-force participation of women, a reduction of the secondary spouse's benefit is being advocated by many on the basis that a 30 percent income differential (rather than the present 50 percent) is all that is required to permit two to maintain the same standard of living as one.

26. See James Schulz's paper in this volume for a discussion of the inadequacies of private pensions.

ments to the wage base and constant wage replacement rates over time may not be necessary. Also they are likely to interfere with private savings.

PRIVATE SAVINGS, CAPITAL FORMATION, AND INTERGENERATIONAL EQUITY

Recently, concern has been raised by some economists that social security is causing a major reduction in private savings and, consequently, having a detrimental effect on the rate of capital formation and the long-term growth rate potential of the economy. Many proponents of this view advocate major payroll tax increases to reduce current consumption, build up large surpluses in the OASDI trust funds, and thereby increase the pool of savings (Feldstein, 1974). These arguments require careful evaluation since they imply a major alteration in the present arrangements for financing social security.

To the extent that the anticipation of receiving social security benefits causes workers to save less toward retirement than they otherwise would, social security does lead to an overall reduction in savings.[27] The evidence is inconclusive on the extent to which this has been occurring;[28] however, even if it has been of minor consequence, it may be of greater magnitude in the future because of the recent rapid growth in social security benefit levels and their expected steady rate of future growth.

If social security actually does reduce private savings by an appreciable amount, should surpluses be built up in the trust funds to offset this effect?[29] In order for the answer to this to be affirmative, two conditions would have to be met: (1) given the projections of

27. This is because the revenues raised through the payroll tax do not represent savings, since they are paid out to beneficiaries (who use most of their social security payments for current consumption) and do not accumulate in a trust fund.

28. Munnell (forthcoming) points out that while using essentially the same data, different estimating techniques have yielded widely different estimates of this effect. According to Munnell, Feldstein concluded that in the absence of social security "1969 personal savings would have been more than double the actual savings figure of $38.2 billion," while her own calculations of the same year found the reduction to be only $3.7 billion. See Feldstein (1974), and Munnell (1974), p. 68, Table 4.7.

Upton (1975), in a review of Munnell's book that also considers Feldstein's analysis, concludes that "firm evidence of a link between social security and the savings rate is lacking."

29. For such a step not to be counterproductive, the total budget surplus (that is considering federal funds plus trust funds) must increase *pari-passu* with the OASDI trust fund surplus, and steps must be taken to maintain full employment, presumably via more expansionary monetary policy since fiscal policy would be constrained.

the effect of OASDI on personal savings, the overall future level of savings in the economy is going to be inadequate to meet desired capital formation needs; and (2) given a need for additional savings, the OASDI trust funds are the best place to accumulate it. Neither of these appears in fact to be the case. On the one hand, the more reliable studies of the capital formation issue indicate that future private savings are unlikely to fall far short of our needs and that we can meet our future capital needs with only minor adjustments in fiscal and monetary policy.[30] And, on the other hand, even if considerable additional savings were required, increased payroll taxes are an undesirable vehicle for accomplishing this. Large rises in payroll taxes on current workers would increase the forced savings of millions of families whose current consumption needs are high relative to their income and who would not choose to increase their savings even at relatively high rates of return. There are many superior alternatives for public action to increase the future savings rate without these adverse distributional consequences.

There is, however, another argument for building up surpluses in the OASDI trust funds which is based on the notion of equity across different generations of workers. If the inflation overadjustment is eliminated in such a manner as to stabilize wage replacement rates over time (Case 4, Table 7–2), then, unless the generation of workers now entering the labor market increases their expected savings rate, financing their future OASDI benefits may require a sharp increase in taxation of the working generations of 2015 and beyond. For this reason it may be desirable to raise taxes for social security for the upcoming generation of workers (with a forgiveness for low-wage workers paid for by general revenues), and build up trust-fund and budget surpluses. The resulting increment in national investment thus could provide some of the wherewithal to moderate the tax impact on the working generation when the upcoming one retires.[31]

CONCLUSIONS

There are two major social security issues that require immediate attention. First, additional funding must be provided to compensate

30. See, for example, Bosworth, Duesenberry, and Carron, (1975), and "Achieving Price Stability" (1974), pp. 93–99.

31. As we indicated earlier, allowing replacement rates to decline is an alternative to higher future revenue requirements. If the burden is going to be placed upon the age cohorts that cause the bulge in the distribution in any event—either through higher taxes to build up budget surpluses or lower benefits—then the choice depends primarily upon the preferred time pattern of consumption of that generation.

for the short-term OASDI deficits. Although this can be postponed for a few more years, it is inevitable. One of the options—raising the wage base—has consequences that are often not fully appreciated. It raises future social security benefits for a population that undoubtedly otherwise would save voluntarily to supplement the smaller social security benefits they would receive. Because it produces higher benefits, raising the wage base has less of a long-run impact on the deficit than it does in the short run, thus necessitating larger future tax increases than other alternatives. And, finally, it further deemphasizes the goal of individual equity at a time when it least can be afforded, by increasing future payroll taxes relative to future benefits for the part of the population that already realizes the lowest rate of return on its "contributions." For these reasons, and because of the distributional impact of the payroll tax, the best means of dealing with the short-term deficit is to gradually shift Medicare to general revenue financing and the present Medicare payroll tax receipts into the OASDI trust funds.

Second, the overadjustment for inflation should be eliminated. Although it has little effect on the short-term deficit, every year this overadjustment continues it adds billions of dollars to the annual amount of the expected long-term deficit and increases the arbitrariness and irrationality of the future benefit structure. Whether the elimination of this inflation overadjustment is accomplished in a way that causes future average benefit levels to rise as fast as or more slowly than real wage growth depends upon judgments about the adequacy of future social security benefits in light of increased potential for voluntary savings and the willingness of upcoming generations to tax themselves. (This latter may be influenced by the fact that another implication of the age shift of the population is that workers will have relatively fewer children to support at the same time there are relatively more aged.) Due to the uncertainty of both the future coverage of private pensions and the exact magnitude of the long-term deficit, it is probably best to provide for stable replacement rates at present with the possibility of allowing them to decline at some future date.[32]

In addition, there are major socioeconomic changes occurring that merit serious analytic attention and public debate on their implications for the future role and structure of social security. The SSI program offers the opportunity to target federal expenditures more

32. Another possibility would be to have the automatic provisions result in declining replacement rates as real wages grow, and to rely upon Congress to make ad hoc upward adjustments in replacement rates if their desirability is indicated.

precisely and broadly on the aged and disabled poor than does OASDI. Middle- and high-wage earners are increasingly gaining access to means of private provision for retirement and disability. These two developments indicate that consideration should be given to social security's playing a more limited future role in a broader system of income support for the aged and disabled that continues over time to provide greater income security protection. Large demographic shifts are also occurring (specifically the rising ratio of beneficiaries to covered workers and increasing labor-force participation of women) which are contributing to inequities within OASDI. All of these changes suggest that a gradual move toward a somewhat more uniform wage replacement rate schedule[33] among different types of beneficiary units and workers at different wage levels may be desirable, as are limitations upon the growth of social security benefits for high-wage workers.

Although it is being advocated by some, concern about our future capital-formation needs does not appear to warrant raising payroll taxes and building surpluses in the trust funds beyond those necessary to provide for a cushion against temporary shortfalls of revenues relative to benefit commitments. It may be desirable, however, if birth rates do not increase substantially, to build up some surpluses in the trust funds in order to more equitably distribute the added financial burden of social security benefits for the post–World War II baby boom generation.

REFERENCES

"Achieving Price Stability through Economic Growth" (1974). Report of the Joint Economic Committee. 93rd Congress, 2nd Session, pp. 93–99.

Brittain, John (1972). *The Payroll Tax for Social Security.* Washington, D.C.: Brookings Institution.

Bosworth, Barry, James S. Duesenberry, and Andrew S. Carron (1975). *Capital Needs in Seventies.* Washington, D.C.: Brookings Institution.

Feldstein, Martin (1974). "Social Security, Induced Retirement, and Aggregate Capital Accumulation," *Journal of Political Economy* 82 (September/October): 905–26.

Henle, Peter (1972). "Recent Trends in Retirement Benefits Related to Earnings," *Monthly Labor Review* [Bureau of Labor Statistics] (June).

33. This refers to the profile of replacement rates within a given cohort of beneficiaries rather than for representative workers of successive (over time) cohorts. Of course, one way of accomplishing this would be to engineer differential rates of change over time in the replacement rates at different points in the profile.

Okner, Ben (1975). "The Social Security Payroll Tax: Some Alternatives for Reform," *Journal of Finance* (May), pp. 567–78.

Munnell, Alicia (forthcoming). *The Future of Social Security.* Washington, D.C.: Brookings Institution.

_____ (1974). *The Effect of Social Security on Personal Savings.* Cambridge: Ballinger Publishing Co.

Palmer, John L., and Joseph J. Minarik (1976). "Income Security Policy," in Henry Owen and Charles Schultze, eds., *Setting National Priorities: The Decade Ahead.* Washington, D.C.: Brookings Institution.

Pechman, Aaron and Taussig (1968). *Social Security: Perspectives for Reform.* Washington, D.C.: Brookings Institution.

Report of the Quadrennial Advisory Council on Social Security (1975). Washington, D.C.: Government Printing Office.

Schulz, James, et al. (1974). *Providing Adequate Retirement Income.* Boston: Brandeis University Press.

Social Security Trustees Report (1976). Washington, D.C.: Government Printing Office.

Thompson, Lawrence (1974). "An Analysis of Factors Currently Determining Benefit Level, Adjustments in Social Security Retirement Program," Technical Analysis Paper No. 1. Office of Income Security Policy, HEW.

U.S. Department of Labor, Bureau of Labor Statistics (1974). *Handbook of Labor Statistics, 1974.* Washington, D.C.: Government Printing Office.

Upton, Charles (1975). "Review of Alicia Munnell's *The Future of Social Security*," *Journal of Political Economy* 83 (October): 1090–92.

Comment on Palmer

R. Harris
T.R. Marmor

There is a growing public debate underway over the future of the social security system in the United States. The debate has been sparked by the realization that the system is both rife with inequities and inadequately financed. So far the debate has not advanced us very far toward serious reform through political action. At the one extreme, defenders of the system are saying that social security will be all right with a few adjustments. At the other, opponents point with either glee or horror to the fact that the system is now substantially underfinanced and argue for scrapping the whole program and (perhaps) starting over again. The latter course of action seems unlikely; the former "minor adjustments" approach will probably prove inadequate. Major changes are needed in the years ahead, and the likely direction of those changes has not yet emerged from the debate.

To reform a program in crisis, it is important to have consensus on the social problems addressed by that program. Only as political actors, agency staffs, intellectual elites, and other divergent interests develop a shared conception of the problems to be solved will it be possible to move in an agreed-upon direction. When there is no such shared conception—and in our view, a clear conception of the social problems to be solved by the social security system has yet to be articulated—we talk past each other. That is now happening in much of the debate over social security.

The welfare reform debate of the 1960s illustrates the importance of problem consensus. A perceived crisis emerged in the welfare debate as new programs and policies emerged to assist the poor during the early 1960s. Within a few years, major welfare reform programs moved very far along toward full implementation. One reason the effort got as far as it did was that a conception of the problem developed reasonably early which could be easily communicated and shared among very diverse groups. In quite abbreviated form, the development can be stated in the following way.[1] First, there was concern about providing adequate incomes to all of the poor, as well as providing adequately for those groups in the population not expected to work. This entailed expanding eligibility for cash transfers to all of the poor, including workers. To do so required concern with work incentives in the welfare system, and led to the development of plans with the structure of a negative income tax. The old conception of the problem addressed by the public assistance system, providing adequately for non-labor-force participants, was replaced by a new one of providing adequately for all of the poor. The new conception necessarily led to very different programmatic thrusts.

In the social security area, old conceptions are breaking down but new ones have not yet emerged. Thus individuals propose "solutions" to the problems they regard as serious, and possible changes are discussed with no consensual standard of relevance at hand. As long as the only real areas of agreement among conceived parties is that (1) the social security program was designed to deal with some of the problems of an economy quite different from that which we seem to be entering; (2) the system no longer fits well; and (3) we are unsure as to what to do, there will be continued discussion of many programmatic changes, floundering with respect to criteria for choice.

We do not have a comprehensive conception of the problem to put forth, nor would our conception necessarily be generally accepted. We will outline, however, what we expect will emerge as elements of social security's new mission.

The social security system was designed at a time when it was expected that marriages would last, and that men would work in the marketplace and women at home, jointly producing household "welfare." It was designed to correspond roughly to a society in which the family with one earner is the basic unit, and to protect family income against some of the circumstances producing loss of earnings by that single earner. Many early features of the social security system make perfect sense in such a society. The same features—wives' benefits for example—seem inequitable in the emerging world, where men and women change partners frequently, and increasingly both spouses expect to work for wages. In our view it would be

1. This history has been explored in book length from three perspectives. See Moynihan (1973); Burke and Vee Burke (1974); and Bowles (1974).

desirable if more of the current debate explicitly concentrated on these social changes, and related the social security system to the needs generated by the current and foreseeable socioeconomic structure, instead of moving directly to the symptoms of the misfit—such as concern for inequities in social security toward women who work or the desirability of a retirement test.

THE PALMER PAPER

Palmer's paper is a contribution to the current debate, but the lack of a general conception of the social security system's past purposes and current dilemmas makes it less useful than we hoped. He covers a number of topics cautiously and competently, outlining the need for a number of changes in social security, and he persuasively shows that some changes must take place. He is convincing that changes are needed, but does not provide a detailed map of the needed changes. Instead, Palmer suggests a few general directions for change. This caution is a virtue of the paper as well as a flaw, since the development of a detailed program of change depends on a clear conception of the current difficulties. Fortunately, the general directions of changes he proposes are appropriate for a range of views of what the ultimate system should look like.

Our major complaint is that his paper does not reflect our views of appropriate balance, and is too blandly uniform in tone. The paper's even tone does not indicate that some of the problems under discussion are profoundly difficult both politically and analytically, while others are relatively trivial. He greatly understates the seriousness of the long-term structural problems in the system, while relatively minor problems are treated as seriously as major ones. In particular, issues dealing with the irrationality of the present benefit structure and with the long-term financial difficulties of the system are dealt with too briefly.

Further, the discussion is improperly constrained by treating the benefit structure within a framework of individual equity based largely upon rate-of-return or benefit/cost calculations. His section on individual equity glosses over many important problems, while twice as much space is devoted to the technically improper way indexing was recently built into the program. The former set of problems requires much analysis, and will be a major source of public debate and political conflict for years, partly because it introduces controversial aspects of social security's purposes. The indexing mistake will be handled much more easily, since it is largely a technical matter where analysts and policy-makers have already reached agreement on the kind of change required.

BENEFIT STRUCTURE AND INDIVIDUAL EQUITY

The structure of benefits under social security is complex and contains many peculiar features. Palmer touches on some of them, but his treatment is constricted considering the immense task facing reformers in the coming years. Policy analysts face the major task of developing appropriate criteria for evaluating social security's benefits. The current emphasis of many economists—focussing on rates of return—is inadequate and less helpful than it seems. Palmer's paper does not exclusively evaluate features of the system in terms of rates of return, but he is fuzzy about other criteria, particularly the concept of social adequacy.

As Palmer notes, the social security system departed from an annuity system very early by conscious acts of policy-makers. Policymakers have typically treated social security as an earmarked tax program to generate revenues to provide a socially (politically) determined set of benefits. As such, it can be viewed as analogous to the gasoline tax, deposited in a highway trust fund and used for road construction. Policy decisions on benefits and eligibility have not been made on the basis of rates of return or benefit/cost ratios. Nor do we expect them to be in a reformed system. While it is useful to calculate such numbers, we should not delude ourselves about their value for dictating future changes. Future changes in benefits will be determined on the basis of criteria of social desirability, or fairness. Rate-of-return calculations do not necessarily provide such criteria. Rates of return—and differences in them--are the *outcome* rather than the objectives of a political process that distributes benefits. Different rates of return for different groups, or for individuals in the system, may or may not be good—depending upon whether or not those differences make sense on the basis of other criteria where notions of equity generally dominate.

Our usual notions of equity hinge on the conception of equal treatment of equals, and unequal treatment of those in unequal circumstances. Equal rates of return do not necessarily follow from such general equity principles. Many of the features of social security that have led to different rates of return were adopted precisely because the circumstances of some beneficiaries were thought to be inappropriately unequal on grounds other than their social security contributions. Higher benefits for married workers and workers with low earning histories in particular were consciously adopted on the presumption of greater need for the income provided. One can envision an equitable system with widely varying rates of return, and vice versa.

We dwell on this point because many recent analyses presented jump from the observation that there are great differences in rates of return to the conclusion that this differentiation indicates inequity. Here, Palmer is somewhat ambivalent. At one point he (correctly) states there is a conflict in the system between individual equity and social adequacy. He then notes that for current workers, the benefit/cost ratio exceeds 1, but that it can be considerably higher for some people. Thus, he concludes, "the social adequacy goal has been pursued to date without having to compromise individual equity at all," because everyone gets a "fair" rate of return. Thus, individual equity is viewed as consistent with unequal rates of return. At other points in his paper, however, he makes arguments that imply that more individual equity in the system calls for greater equality in benefit/cost ratios. This is a tricky point, and we urge great caution in using rate-of-return calculations as anything other than measurements of differences in treatment, which require further exploration to see if they are justified.

With that said, let us note that we believe the present benefit system is inequitable, and that some of the inequities can be illuminated by rate-of-return differences that do seem senseless by other criteria. We believe that the system has developed in its present form because policy-makers assumed that creating categories of benefits and beneficiaries on the basis of presumed need would not raise profound problems. It was envisaged that:

1. Population and labor force would continue to grow into the far distant future, generating more and more "contributors."
2. Real income would continue to grow at a high rate.
3. The social security tax rate and taxable wage base would both continue to rise.

This is roughly the way social security has worked for the past 40 years, making it easy periodically to liberalize benefits and eligibility. Providing larger benefits to the aged, survivors, and the disabled involved almost no perceived political costs in the 1960s. In making incremental changes in benefits and coverage to allocate increments of dollars among current and prospective new beneficiary classes, rate-of-return calculations did not play much of a role—in part perhaps because it was assumed that everyone's benefit/cost ratio would far exceed 1. Many such decisions were made on the basis of the presumed need of particular groups, with full knowledge that their rate of return would be very high. The issue of concern for many has been the adequacy of a pension relative to some measured preretirement income, or simply post-retirement need, rather than cumulative contributions.

The demographic and economic changes now taking place, which Palmer mentions, make it increasingly likely that benefit/cost ratios will not exceed 1 for everybody in the future. Put another way, we cannot afford to maintain the current benefit structure unless we are prepared to accept very large increases in the payroll tax, or devote significant amounts of general revenues to the system. (The latter alternative is not costless, since it requires higher than otherwise needed taxes, or that other public expenditures be lower.) The new environment of fiscal stringency also makes many of the past decisions to provide considerably higher rates of return for some groups than others appear more inequitable than they were originally. Moreover, in the past when "inequities" (however defined) were noted, we could console ourselves that they would be remedied in the future—because revenues would be available to eliminate them by bringing benefits of the disadvantaged up, or by providing general increases that would swamp the identified discriminations. Now we must consider remedying inequities by bringing down benefits which are "too high," or selectively retarding growth in benefits. Politically, this is much more difficult. A great deal of detailed analysis will be necessary to spark the sort of public debate essential for political consensus on the changes that must over the long run be made.

While we agree with the tenor of Palmer's general directions for change, we feel he has not sufficiently explained his reasoning to the policy world, and that much more detailed analyses of all the features of the current benefit structure need to be conducted prior to developing a specific program of long-range change. Examples of features that should be analyzed carefully are discussed in the following paragraphs.

1. The minimum benefit and minimum eligibility requirements. Easy eligibility for a minimum benefit has been justified on the basis of presumed need. But one reason for low covered earnings, leading to a very high return on contribution, is marginal attachment to the social security system rather than low earnings. Federal government workers who acquire social security coverage through moonlighting or post-retirement private-sector employment are usually pointed out as individuals for whom a very high rate of return is inappropriate (as opposed to the long-term very low-wage worker). Palmer notes that

many local governments are dropping out of the system, and thus this problem will get worse.

2. Benefits to surviving children of a deceased worker end at age 18, but if the child remains in school, they can continue to age 21. Thus, the rate of return on the worker's contribution depends essentially on whether the children attend college. This scholarship program is unique in that no test of financial need or good scholarship is attached to it, and it should be reviewed carefully. Should this feature continue in a world of fiscal stringency?

3. Working wives and single workers are discriminated against in that they receive a much lower rate of return than married couples in which only one spouse works. (The rate of return for working wives can approach zero.) These benefit differences were adopted on the basis of presumed need, but the basis for that presumption is steadily getting weaker. It is not clear that these differentials are appropriate in a system with relatively high wage replacement rates, and, as Palmer notes, a world in which a significant and growing proportion of workers are accumulating rights to other pension benefits. In a world in which most women work and are no longer in general expected to live exclusively on men's earnings, the payment of a wife's benefit with no test of need will become an anachronism.

Many other features could be similarly flagged. Some of these can be flagged by noting (questionably) different rates of return to groups. We suspect that most could be flagged as easily in the system if it were fully financed by general revenues, so that rate-of-return calculations could not sensibly be made.

SKIPOVERS

A number of other points are skipped over in Palmer's paper with inadequate analysis or exposition. A few are worth mentioning briefly.

SSI, Rates-of-Return, and "Net" Benefits of Social Security: We have been somewhat critical of reliance on a rate-of-return conception of social security's equity. But if one uses such an evaluative standard, the newly implemented Supplemental Security Income (SSI) program raises a problem Palmer skips over. SSI provides for disregarding the first $20 of social security income in calculating cash benefits, and then reduces SSI benefits dollar-for-dollar for additional social security income. For many current and future workers, a net social security benefit of $20 is all they will receive regardless of their contributions. For those whose earned benefits range from zero to the SSI maximum plus $20, the "tax rate" on social security benefits above $20 is 100 percent. From a benefit/cost perspective, this means social security has become, in net terms, a worse buy for lower-income workers than it was prior to the enactment of SSI. Tolley and Burkhauser touched on this issue in their paper, but primarily highlighted its undesirable implications for early retirement.

Attributing Social Security Contributions to Worker and Spouse: Palmer suggests in passing a solution that bears both on the working vs. nonworking wife topic and the fair treatment of single workers. "Crediting half of the sum of a husband's and wife's earnings to each," he suggests, would permit phasing out of the secondary spouse's benefit while helping the minority of wives who work in the home by giving them credit for half their spouse's earnings. This is an interesting suggestion worth far more analysis and discussion. Among other things, it may be a reasonable way of dealing with the impact of divorce on women married to the same man for less than twenty years. Under current law, such women receive full spouse's benefits after twenty years of marriage, and nothing otherwise unless they themselves have worked.

The Politics of Social Security/Policy Change: Palmer generally avoids comment on the character of social security politics, as is appropriate in a paper stressing economic aspects of the system. Where he does mention the origins of change, he implicitly assumes that social security policy change emerges from dispassionate consideration of problems with current operations. Following this view, policy changes that have taken place must have resulted from the program's problems; future problems will prompt policy response on the same logic. The task of analysts, then, is to get the right reform for the problems sensible people have noted. This is not an ambitious enough goal for serious policy analysts and we must do more.

A good example of this perspective is Palmer's unselfconscious account of benefit indexation in the early 1970s as it appears on p. 158, above:

> In order to insure that current beneficiaries' payments keep pace with inflation, and in an attempt to prevent the need for continued ad hoc adjustments in the revenue structure, Congress incorporated into the social security system a set of automatic adjustments which went into effect in 1974.

Yet these problems antedated the early 1970s, the concept of indexing was well known, and it was much discussed at HEW and in Congress earlier. But Congress did not act, presumably because it preferred to explicitly make "ad hoc adjustments" periodically.

The reasons analysts regard as justification for a course of action may not be the reasons why action is taken. Thus, when we identify all of the problems in the social security system that need reform, we may be a long way from understanding how to make it happen. In addition to the economic analysis, we must study the political forces that dictate either change or continuity in important policy areas, lest ignoring those forces drive us away from solutions to some of the problems we identify, or defer Congress's willingness to address the serious long-run problems that are inherent in the current system. The sooner the problems are explicitly addressed politically, the easier will be the solutions—because deferring action creates new privileges under a conflicted system.

REFERENCES

Burke, Vincent J., and Vee Burke (1974). *Nixon's Good Deed: Welfare Reform.* New York: Columbia University Press.

Bowles, Kenneth (1974). *The Nixon Guaranteed Income Proposal: Substance and Process in Policy Change.* Cambridge, Mass.: Ballinger Publishing Company.

Moynihan, Daniel P. (1973). *The Politics of a Guaranteed Income: The Nixon Administration and the Family Assistance Plan.* New York: Random House.

Chapter 8

Overview

Werner Z. Hirsch

Critical commentaries on the present state and future health of the U.S. social security system have been appearing with increasing regularity during the past few years. Different writers have voiced varied grounds for concern, and with differing urgency. Barbara Koeppel (1976) expresses a popular view that "growing old does not mean entering the serene secure years for most Americans. The old are often abused, frequently cheated, and financially deprived despite the promise of social security. . . . Social Security benefits even with Medicare are inadequate." She finds the source of all evil in "the original design of the Social Security Program (which) almost insured that it would be inadequate and unfair, with workers and the poor carrying a disproportionate share of the burden of the elderly. . . . Social Security in this country shapes up as one of the nation's most regressive programs . . ."

This view is strongly contradicted herein by Laffer and Ranson. They invoke a morality argument that "a failure to satisfy the necessary economic and financial criteria would also be deficient on humanitarian criteria," as well as an economic argument, and urge us to reverse the trend social security has been following in recent years. Laffer and Ranson express alarm not only about the size of the prospective deficits, but also about anti-work biases, and about the manner in which the system mixes the individual equity aspect of an insurance scheme with distributive social adequacy considerations. Somewhere in between these extremes falls John Palmer's paper which, while finding inequities within the program, points to "the feasibility and desirability of social security playing a more limited future role in the overall income support picture for the retired and severely disabled workers and their families." But even Palmer is concerned about deficits in the next ten years, and in the long term. Similar middle ground is staked out by James Morgan.

In spite of the three papers vocalizing in different keys, they have much in common. To begin with, there is wide agreement that our income-support policy for the aging lacks clear purpose; as James Morgan puts it, "We do need clearer logic to justify the system and set its parameters." Agreement on a precise specification of the objective function of the social security system is essential because "the goal of social adequacy is [in] . . . conflict with that of individual equity." There is widespread agreement about the desirability of a more careful sorting out of these two objectives, though the authors differ about the importance to be assigned to the second objective. Laffer and Ranson favor divorcing the social security system from social adequacy considerations altogether. Future benefits should be based on contributions alone, thus ruling out use of general tax moneys. While their credo is "to provide an economically sound and efficient system that satisfies society's revealed preference to provide a better life for the aged," they say nothing about those aged who are in poverty. Even while unemployed, participants would be expected to pay their insurance premium and, depending on how little they had paid in, their benefits at retirement could be quite small.

Morgan's view differs, if for no other reason than that he looks at the social security fund within a macroeconomic setting. He determines that general federal taxes should finance parts of the social security system. His economic reasons are that "the capital investment that past nonconsuming due to social security taxes allowed has increased productivity of both labor and capital, and there is justification for using federal income taxes, personal and corporate, to provide that interest return on the 'investments.' " Palmer sees the beginnings of efforts at separating out the redistribution component from the social security system. Specifically, he points to the Supplemental Security Income program, a new federal guaranteed income program for the aged and disabled. If this program were developed to meet the social adequacy goal, then the social security system could return to an emphasis on sound individual equity.

There is some disagreement between Morgan and Palmer about what the appropriate real rate of return on payroll tax contributions should be. The former suggests 3 and the latter 2 percent, which he claims to "be considered fair by most . . . [and] somewhat higher than savings accounts yielded on average over the past sixty years."

Since present legislation assures that increases in the cost of living are doubly reflected in the relative benefits granted to successive cohorts of retirees, all three papers favor the immediate elimination of this "coupling."

Laffer and Ranson agree with Morgan that the present income test should be changed. Clearly, in a Laffer-Ranson system that implements the principle of "dollar-in-dollar-out," any income test is inappropriate. Morgan merely calls for a modified income test. He would wave the income test, for example, if persons over 65 were to work in jobs "serving community needs." While the sentiment is commendable, we must realize the difficulty of effectively defining such a class of jobs and policing performance to meet the spirit of the classification.

We have empirical evidence that appears to indicate that the income test has a great influence on retirement decisions. For example, Boskin's econometric work suggests that a decrease in the implicit tax rate on earnings from one-half to one-third would reduce the annual probability of retirement by almost 60 percent (Boskin, 1975). Therefore, a change in the social security system that increases employment of the aged must be examined in the light of the broader employment policies to be pursued during the next decades. Moreover, we need to know more about the cross-elasticity of the demand for aged and nonaged workers before policy decisions can be reached.

The argument about what, if any, is an optimum income test for the aged brings me to an issue that has left me with some discomfort. Virtually all discussions look at the social security system in isolation. There are some exceptions, and some of these are concerned with savings. But they are still an exception. I would like to illustrate my concern in relation to two further examples.

First, there is the dollar-in-dollar-out principle that has been proposed. Let us remember that we are speaking of very large annual flows into and out of the social security fund. Will political and macroeconomic considerations tolerate an actuarially sound collection and disbursement system? Why should or could we expect the fate of the payroll tax, particularly now that it amounts to about 10 percent of wages, to be very different from that of the federal income tax? The social security fund is so large that macroeconomic effects cannot be neglected. Once a fund has reached so large a size, it is virtually impossible to retain the sole objective of an insurance program and neglect the political temptation and perhaps economic wisdom to manipulate it over time in order to bring about economic stability.

My second example relates to the debate whether the present social security system is and should be regressive or progressive. There is general agreement that the payroll tax system becomes highly regressive beyond a certain income level. This is readily seen from Pechman's income incidence data for 1966, regardless of the incidence assumptions made (Pechman, 1974). Thus, up to the income group that coincides with the maximum individual earnings base, the tax is mildly progressive, and from then on it turns strongly regressive. However, we must distinguish between a differential incidence calculation of the sort made by Pechman, and a budget incidence analysis that considers the combined effects of the payroll tax and the payout and expenditure changes that result. The expenditure side has its direct effects on private income of the aged, and indirect effects on those who are secondary and tertiary recipients of these moneys of the aged. Moreover, the intergeneration effects of the social security system should be considered in a broader setting that takes into consideration other intergeneration effects, such as financing of public education for the young.

Thus, while it would be unreasonable to expect that an income-support program for the aging could solve also many others of the world's great problems, it is reasonable to insist that it be so designed as not to create major new problems or exacerbate existing ones. The latter could happen, for instance, if as suggested by Moon and Smolensky we were to measure the economic well-being of the aged to include intrafamily financial support. It could induce children and other relatives to reduce financial assistance for aged relatives, since such help would reduce government support. Likewise, Moon and Smolensky's suggested actuarial mortgage plans, which would permit the aged to transfer ownership of their homes to some intermediary while retaining rent-free residence for life, could have some deleterious side effects. It could further reduce incentives of aging families to move to smaller homes—preferably apartments which are easier to take care of and where it is easier to take care of them, and whereby more efficient use is made of the nation's housing stock.

It would be a serious mistake to attribute all of the contemporary discontent with the social security system to its fuzzy objectives. The scarcity of econometric inquiries and the absence of a powerful economic theory, which could tackle the problem within a general equilibrium setting, contribute to the present situation in which the social security system has become an object of discontent and concern for the future.

But even lacking such information, the papers and deliberations of the conference appear to justify the following considerations.

Existing income-support programs for the aging constitute an unholy mixture of various components, some of which rely on the benefit principle and others on the ability-to-pay principle. Superimposed on the social security system, and not fitting too well, is the relatively new Supplemental Security Income program designed to offer federal income support for the aged and disabled. There are indications that funds could be used with much greater cost effectiveness if we would move toward two separate but complementary systems, one using the benefit principle and the other the ability-to-pay principle. The former should come as close as possible to being collection and payout neutral. The second could be a modification and extension of the Supplemental Security Income program which, in the absence of a general income-maintenance program, should provide income maintenance for the aged. Not only is this a desirable direction for long-run improvements, but also for curing the short-run insolvency of the social security system. As Lawrence Thompson has shown, the 20 percent of social security recipients who also qualified for Supplemental Security Income benefits in 1973 were paid from social security about $3.7 billion, that is, about 8 percent of all annual social security retirement and survivor payments. This amount is more than twice the $1.6 billion paid out by the new federal Supplemental Security Income program.

Implementing such changes would also go a long way toward removing what amounts to a serious threat to the survival of the system. Much publicity has recently been given to the liquidity and solvency problems of the social security system. Also, more and more members of the middle- and upper-income classes appear to realize that the ability-to-pay element has become increasingly important in the system. Perhaps in response to these two issues, state and local governments have begun to seriously consider contracting out of it.[1] Since state and local governments employ close to 15 percent of U.S. workers, wholesale desertion could become an immediate threat to the system.

Moreover, private and public unions in recent years have written into their contracts generous private retirement programs. As a result, important parts of our labor force are likely to exceed what might be considered an optimum retirement program. The drawback would be excessively heavy contributions toward their retirement. Regard-

1. A total of 322 state and local government units with about 45,000 employees have dropped out of the social security system since they came under its provisions in 1956. At the present time another 232 government units employing 454,000 have given the required two-year notice that they intend to pull out.

less of whether the costs of these contributions are ultimately borne by employers or are shifted to employees and customers of their products, the costs of goods and services are likely to rise and the incentives of workers to work and save will be reduced.

If the thoughtful papers that were presented here today begin to disentangle a most complicated and, in many respects, irrational set of retirement programs, and separate them into more cost-effective and side-effect neutral components, an important contribution will have been made.

REFERENCES

Boskin, Michael (1975). "Social Security and Retirement Decisions." National Bureau of Economic Research, Workshop on Pension Research, May.

Koeppel, Barbara (1976). "How America's Elderly Get Short-Changed," *Los Angeles Times*, April 18.

Pechman, Joseph (1974). *Who Bears the Tax Burden?* Washington, D.C.: Brookings Institution.

About the Editors

George S. Tolley is Professor of Economics at the University of Chicago and co-chairman of the University's Program on Resources of the Committee on Public Policy. He served as Deputy Assistant Secretary for Tax Policy of the U.S. Treasury in 1974 and 1975. Prior to joining the Chicago faculty in 1966, he was with the U.S. Department of Agriculture where he was responsible for economic development of non-metropolitan parts of the economy.

Dr. Tolley received his M.A. and Ph.D. degrees from the University of Chicago. He taught at North Carolina University and was a Visiting Professor at the University of California, Berkeley and at Purdue University. From 1965 to 1966, he was Vice President of the American Farm Economic Association. He is the author or editor of numerous publications and has been associated with societies and associations covering broad spectrums of activities. Dr. Tolley is a member of numerous committees and consultant to organizations and government commissions related to his areas of interest. His fields of research and writing include agricultural economics, economic development, urban economics, natural resources and environmental problems, monetary fiscal policy and consumer demand.

Richard V. Burkhauser is an economist. His primary interests are in applied price theory and labor economics. For the past few years he has been involved in research on the problems of the aged. His publications in this area include "Federal Economic Policy Toward the Elderly" and "The Early Pension Decision and Exit from the

Labor Market." Mr. Burkhauser is a research associate at the Institute for Research on Poverty, University of Wisconsin–Madison and is currently on leave to the Office of Income Security Policy, Department of Health, Education, and Welfare.